Praise for *Role Re*

D0192231

"Iris Waichler delicately describes the nature of life struggle as we get older. She not only describes how to be an advocate for your parents but also fulfilling that role as daughter. This book is sure to help in the understanding of words like 'hospice' and 'Alzheimer's.' It addresses living wills, estate planning, driving concerns, adult day enhancement, nursing homes, and just what to expect during the mortal nature of living. More than anything though, it reflects on decline such that dignity may be preserved. This book is certain to lift your spirits, raise your intellect, and contribute to the purpose behind giving back to what parents give their children."

— Steven Atkinson PA-C, MS Geriatric Internal Medicine,
Adjunct Faculty-University of Utah

"*Role Reversal* does a beautiful job of intertwining personal experience with professional guidance. Her professional background working with older adults, combined with her long and loving relationship with her father, make her uniquely qualified to provide insight and support. With every page her father comes alive as the spirited, driven, and devoted person that he was. His story is an inspiration. This highly readable book will leave you feeling like you know Ms. Waichler and her father well. It will also gift you with resources and guidance as you engage with your parent in later life."

— Susan Alterman, Psy/D, licensed clinical psychologist

"Iris Waichler did a beautiful job covering the various aspects and challenges related to becoming a caregiver. From the emotional and financial stresses, to the decision-making process and paperwork, caregiving can be overwhelming. This book takes a unique approach by sharing one man's incredible story while simultaneously preparing readers for the unexpected and offering resources and guidance to ease the transition."

— B. Popper, Account Director

Published 2016
Printed in the United States of America
ISBN: 978-1-63152-091-4 pbk
ISBN: 978-1-63152-092-1 ebk
Library of Congress Control Number: 2016935741

Cover design by Julie Metz Ltd./metzdesign.com
Interior design by Tabitha Lahr

For information, address:
She Writes Press
1563 Solano Ave #546
Berkeley, CA 94707

She Writes Press is a division of SparkPoint Studio, LLC.

Role Reversal

How to Take Care
of Youself and
Your Aging Parents

IRIS WAICHLER, MSW, LCSW

SHE WRITES PRESS

Contents

PART TWO

Dedication

This book was conceived as I watched my loving and lovable father, Melvin Edward Sneider, advance in age. I began to assume a larger role in his life, helping him when he asked, and later even when he didn't. He needed the help even though he didn't know it.

As I began sharing my idea about this book, I met so many people who began telling stories of becoming caregivers for their loved ones. I heard their stories of the good and bad and everything the role entails.

I dedicate this book to my father, who vowed to never be a burden and did the best he could to take care of his family and himself every day of his life. I also dedicate my book to the millions of people who are or have been caregivers for their family or friends. Your challenges may feel overwhelming at times; some days they certainly are. Hopefully, along the way you will experience the rewards that can come with this role. Always remember that you are not alone. Caregivers need to be able to ask for help. My goal for this book is to remind you there are people and places you can turn to.

Many of us may ultimately need the kindness of a caregiver some day. And I hope there is someone in your life that will be there to take on that role when you need it the most.

Introduction

The Challenges—and Rewards—of the Parental Role Reversal

The phone rang at 11:00 P.M. and immediately jolted me awake. Those of us with elderly parents know the uneasy feeling when an unexpected call awakens us late at night. I jumped up and hurried to the phone.

It was a nurse at my father's assisted-living facility. Dad had fallen. "I think you should come over right away," she told me.

I was out the door and in my car in five minutes, going as fast as I could on the ten-minute drive to Dad's place. I was thinking about him and how he had done all he could to take care of himself and be independent. He had been so strong and capable when my siblings and I were growing up. Over the years, he'd faced—and overcome—many challenges. He continued to amaze us with his humor and ability to rebound.

I got to his apartment. I could hear a woman laughing on the other side of the door. When I walked in, Dad was sitting on his couch in his underwear and bathrobe. His right arm and leg were covered in blood. And he was holding the nurse's hand, shamelessly flirting with her.

"Listen, doll," he said, "I think I'm gonna make it, don't you?" She smiled at us both, and assured me that he was okay.

Dad had fallen in his bathroom, grabbing the towel bar on the way down. He'd banged his leg and arm against the tub. Luckily he'd been aware enough to pull the emergency cord in his bathroom to get help.

"What about his injuries?" I asked her. "And his vital signs?" She told me he was fine.

His vital signs were just slightly elevated. But neither she nor my dad could explain exactly why he fell.

"Your dad is quite a joker," she told me cheerfully.

I spent the night sleeping on the floor at Dad's apartment, having been unable to get comfortable on his little couch. I knew he'd get up around 4:00 A.M. This had been his routine for over seventy years, and I wanted to make sure there were no more falls. It took me a long time to fall asleep. Lying there, I thought about how lucky my siblings and I were that Dad had been doing so well for such a long time. But I also began considering what additional safeguards we would need to put into place. Our goal was to keep Dad as safe and as healthy as possible.

When I began writing this book, my dad was ninety-six

years old. My sisters and brother and I were betting that he would reach the century mark. Dad continued to work out three times a week. His only complaint then was that his legs were feeling weaker and he couldn't walk as far as he used to. All in all, he was in remarkably good health.

Every year when we'd celebrate his birthday, I thanked him for doing such a great job of taking care of himself. "Keep up the good work, Dad," I'd say playfully.

He always smiled and replied, "I keep doing the best I can." And he did. We were all so grateful for him. We all loved him. He was such a large presence in my life that I couldn't imagine him ever not being a part of it.

That night, after Dad's fall, as I lay on the floor, tossing and turning, I thought about my daughter, Grace, who was seven at the time. Many of us have parents who, as they grow older, need more and more help from their adult children. Grace will probably take on that role one day for my husband and me. This is the way it goes for every new generation.

Every day each of us grows older. As our bodies age, our physical and mental abilities change. Sometimes this process moves slowly. It can also shift in dramatic and unwelcome ways.

There are no magic cures or means to stop the aging process. Cosmetic surgery changes what's on the outside but not what's on the inside. Medical interventions at key times can offer some relief and stabilization. And along the way, family, friends, and/or health-care professionals may need to step in to offer assistance. Sometimes seniors treasure this assistance. At other times, they are less receptive.

Some seniors may stubbornly object to any type of intervention. This can happen despite the obvious necessity that those close to them can see.

As we live our lives, we collect stories about what we experience. Each of us has our own unique collection of stories that make us who we are. Our history influences the choices we make later in our lives. We all have a need to be heard; we all want to live our lives as we see fit regardless of our age. We want people to take the time to listen, respect, and understand these decisions.

It is a blessing for all concerned when those involved in the caretaking process agree on a course of action to support their loved ones as they grow older. Many of us will later look back at these critical junctures in the lives of our seniors, and reflect upon what happened. Ideally we will believe that the right decisions were made to keep them as healthy, independent, and safe as possible. But in the here and now, many caretakers are focusing on helping their aging parents maintain as rich a day-to-day existence as can be managed. Sometimes, taking the time to think about their past can give us important clues as to how best to tackle the challenges in the present.

If it's possible and you haven't done so already, I encourage you to listen to your parents' rendering of their own living history, and to ask them about what they want, both now and in the future. Hearing their stories can take us to places we have never been. It brings that history alive. These stories can inspire us and teach us about how we came to be who we are.

Often, seniors will repeat anecdotes and tales; they

might forget or confuse the details. We can still learn much from what they tell us. Even if your parent tells you a story you've heard many times before, perhaps asking a new question will divulge a new perspective or detail that captures both your attention and your imagination. And this additional understanding can offer fresh insight that helps us to be better caretakers.

All families have a unique history. If we're lucky, stories of our ancestors have been shared from generation to generation. One of the favorite parts of my work as a medical social worker was taking the time to hear the life histories of my elderly patients. I tried to incorporate that in my work with them and in their discharge planning. Often, they were eager to talk with me because few others took the time to listen. In many instances they had repeated these stories so many times to family or friends that they were not interested in hearing them.

As I came to see over the years, these life biographies share common themes. Seniors will frequently describe ancestors coming to this country to create a new life, striving to create families and fulfill dreams. Their themes as they talk are similar. They talk about work, falling in love, sickness, money, family, tears, triumphs, failures, and relationships that shaped their lives. Another theme from these stories is war. Veterans from World War II still can be eager to tell their tales. Sadly, we are losing these veterans at a rate of three hundred per day.

As you read this book, I encourage you to think about how the themes of these stories relate to your aging loved ones. At the same time, what do you see happening with them in their day-to-day lives? Who are they now; and who were they? How does the past affect their relationships today?

As I was writing this section, I couldn't help but think about how relevant these questions are for our brave soldiers of today. Coming home, many of them are wounded both physically and emotionally—just as veterans have always been.

Soldier or not, as we move through our adulthood, all of us experience the themes I describe above. We must face our own individual aging process and make choices about how to engage in our daily lives. Inevitably, we bring our histories into our current lives and our relationships; having an awareness of this can shape us for the better.

The numbers on aging are changing. We are living longer than ever before. According to the 2010 census, "There are 53,364 centenarians living in the United States and these numbers continue to increase." The term "silver tsunami" has been used to describe the growing population of people who are now living well into their nineties and beyond. In fact, according to a study by the Gerontology Research Group, there are sixty-eight people—whom they call "supercentenarians"—whose ages the Group has validated to be 110 or more, and "they estimate the real number is closer to three hundred to four hundred and fifty persons."

The Pew Research Center reports that in response to our parents living longer, there's been a proportionate increase in the number of adults assuming caregiver roles. They reported that this "is especially prevalent among adults ages thirty to sixty-four, a group traditionally still in the workforce." Their "statistics show an increase in caregivers rising from 30 percent in 2010 to 39 percent in 2013."

Unfortunately, this role reversal doesn't come easily for all concerned. As adult children, there's a lot to think about when we become our parents' caretakers and must confront this radical shifting of responsibilities.

Reactions vary. Sometimes we talk awkwardly with our parents. We struggle to create new boundaries. Sometimes there are raging battles among siblings about who is going to do what—battles which can end up destroying lifelong relationships.

Identifying and assessing your parent's needs and who will fulfill the necessary caregiver responsibilities takes determination, patience, knowledge, and—all too often— money. It includes a wide-ranging set of skills that few of us initially have.

At the heart of the personal narrative in this book is the story of my father and the evolution of our family. His need for assistance as he grew older is reflected in so many families today. I realized that there are literally thousands of people just like me who struggle to understand and get a handle on the reversal of roles that takes place as we begin to be caretakers for our parents.

I've been a licensed clinical social worker for over thirty-five years. Much of my career was as a medical social worker, working with elderly people who'd been admitted to the hospital. A big part of my job was advocacy. I made sure that my patients and their families understood their medical condition and treatment goals. I encouraged them to talk with health-care professionals when they had questions or concerns. My work also included helping manage the discharge planning for these patients and their families.

Along with sharing my dad's story I've included useful information to help guide you through the challenges of assuming this new caregiver role. Most chapters in Part One feature a personal narrative followed by key caregiver guidelines, expert insights, and resource material.

Part Two is devoted exclusively to the major challenges that caregivers face, such as how to manage hospital bills and insurance questions, dividing up caretaker responsibilities, choosing a nursing home, and estate planning. It contains a wide array of information, including links to additional governmental, nonprofit, and private resources.

Writing this book has been truly a labor of love. It's taken me in directions I would not have imagined when I began it. I did a lot of research, which offered new revelations. I was surprised by the number of people who found themselves in this position. I was also struck by the fact that often they didn't know how to access information and resources that could help. And their sense of isolation and helplessness could be immobilizing.

In my role as author there may be names or specific details I chose not to include in order to protect and respect the privacy of certain individuals or events. But everything you'll read about my dad's family history is the truth as far as I know it. It's based on my own observations over the years as well as the stories and anecdotes shared by my parents, other relatives, and friends.

In my family, Dad was famous for the sayings he would

have ready for all occasions. He had a wonderful sense of humor, which only grew sharper as he aged. When he would make an outrageous comment or observation, my siblings and I would often tease him about it. Inevitably Dad would smile, and he'd reply firmly, his eyes twinkling, "I only say it because it's true." That was his mantra and it will be mine to you, the reader, throughout this book.

Although my family's story is unique, I am certain that along the way there will be situations that will be familiar to you and your loved ones. My hope is that by writing about my experiences and what I've learned, you'll find valuable clarity and support. If you're feeling overwhelmed by the challenges of helping your elderly loved one, I hope that this book will enable you to face them with new insight and energy. Remember, you are not alone.

Iris Waichler with her father, Melvin, on her wedding day in 1996.

PART ONE

Chapter 1

The Early Years

Coping with Grief and Loss of Family

In 2009, when my dad was ninety years old, I went to visit him in his apartment at his assisted-living facility. It was a short ten-minute drive I would make every week, or more if necessary. He handed me several sheets of paper, filled with handwritten notes, and said, "I decided to write down my life story."

I was surprised. Dad wasn't usually a reflective person, and had never written anything remotely autobiographical, so this was very out of character. "What motivated you to do this, Dad?" I asked him.

"I've been thinking about it, and I wanted to get it all down before I'm gone," he answered. "I want you to read it all."

I looked at the first paragraph.

I am six years of age and am scheduled to attend first grade at the Haugen School. My parents designate my brother Jules for the task. He is five years older than me. He takes me to the school yard and deserts me. It is winter and I am cold, lonely, frightened, and lost. After many lonely hours I find my way home. How I don't know. My parents pay little attention to me.

This stark incident of being abandoned by his brother forever dominated Dad's memories of growing up. It was linked to his feelings about his parents, too. He believed they were aware of the cruelty inflicted by Jules, but did nothing to intervene. Even in his nineties he still had dreams of being lost as a little boy—lost and unable to find his way back home.

Many of Dad's recollections of his childhood and youth were tinged with sadness and loneliness. He would talk about the lack of love or support from anyone in his immediate family.

In addition to his older brother Jules, Dad had a younger sister, Edith. He also had a stepbrother, Sidney, who was ten years older than he was. Not only would Dad describe the emotional abuse directed at him by his father, Harry, he said that Sidney was subjected to physical abuse from Harry because there wasn't a biological relationship between them.

Harry and his wife, Sarah—my grandmother—had emigrated from Russia. They came to the United States through Ellis Island. When Harry was being processed

Melvin had a troubled relationship with his parents Sarah and Harry Sneider.

through immigration services, they asked him if his name was spelled "Schneider." It was actually "Sneider," but unable to read or write in English, and not knowing what else to do, Harry simply said yes. (Many years later, Dad persuaded him to legally change his name back to Sneider. I think Dad was embarrassed by his illiteracy and felt strongly about setting the record straight.)

Unlike my grandfather Harry, my grandmother Sarah was a well-educated woman. She had divorced her first husband and had a young son—Sidney—to take care of. She never spoke about her first husband to my dad, so I never learned anything about him or why they split up. It must have been something significant, though, for her to strike out on her own.

Both of Dad's parents lived with us during my childhood. It seemed to me that my grandmother was afraid of my grandfather. This dovetails with later discussions I had with Dad, who believed that Sarah was grateful to have found a man willing to marry a divorcée with a young child, and that she was afraid that if she took a stand in any way opposing my grandfather, she would be jeopardizing her marriage— something she was unwilling to risk after going through one divorce. Still, Dad blamed her for not speaking up when my grandfather was cruel to the boys in the family; he never forgave her passive behavior whenever Harry yelled, called them names, or struck them when he got angry at some perceived infraction of his rules. And yet, Dad said, he and Jules never stopped competing for positive attention from their parents.

To the end, Dad believed with enormous resentment that Jules was "the favorite son," and that Edith was treated as a favored child because she was a girl and the youngest. It was a lot of emotional baggage for him to carry his whole life.

Dad grew up in a poor neighborhood in Chicago, Illinois. His father, Harry, traveled up and down the alleys in a horse-drawn cart, searching for junk and scrap metal that he could sell. This was how he supported his family.

Later Harry had enough money to purchase an old truck, and over time his business improved enough for him to move his family to a new neighborhood called Albany Park. Dad was twelve years old at that time. It was a move up into a better home and what he hoped would be a better life.

In his little autobiography, Dad describes a traumatic incident that happened after their move to Albany Park:

> One day Sidney puts a can on Jules's head and
> decided to shoot it off with a gun. I know this is a

subtle method to murder him and I put a stop to it.
Instead Sid talks Jules into entering a wooden barrel
and puts a .22-caliber bullet through the barrel hole,
which enters Jules hand just beneath the surface of
the skin. I dig it out for fear that Pa will punch Sid.

This protective instinct explains a lot about my dad back then and throughout his life. Despite the emotional complexity of his home life growing up, Dad still had an incredibly strong sense of the importance of family. This, juxtaposed with his innately strong feelings about right and wrong, fostered a powerful urge to help his relatives, just as he did with his brothers during that long-ago incident, risking the wrath of his father in this act of kindness. My dad would forgive many perceived injustices against him—both when he was a child and when he was an adult—that were committed by all of his immediate family members over the years. Still, with Dad, forgiving by no means meant forgetting what had transpired.

I recall my grandfather Harry as a quiet, distant man, who rarely smiled or showed much physical affection. I don't remember seeing any signs of affection displayed between him and my dad in the many years he lived with us. Harry was a heavyset man; he had bushy eyebrows, and thick creases in his face that showed the passage of the years. He would often sit in the living room with the newspaper held out in front of him, but it was upside down. As I grew older, I realized that he was pretending to read in front of me and my sister Susie. Appearances were important to him. At the time, we didn't understand why he needed to create that charade.

Despite his illiteracy, Harry successfully ran his scrap-metal business. Dad worked in the warehouse with him. They were long, very physically demanding days. Dad also dealt directly with the customers and helped with the bookkeeping. And he did the inventory work along with the reading and writing of contracts to help conceal his father's limitations. They got some help from Jules. But Jules wasn't willing to consistently put in the hours or the physical labor that was a part of the job, such as lifting and moving huge three-hundred-pound barrels full of different types of metals.

As for my grandmother Sarah, I remember her as a quiet woman, small and fragile. She followed my grandfather around the house, like his shadow, and would sit with him in the living room. She'd give Susie and me a hug or a kiss sometimes, but, like Harry, didn't talk very much to us. They both assumed passive roles within our household. My mother was responsible for making sure they were fed, their clothes were cleaned, and they got the proper medical care when necessary.

Sarah died from cancer when she was seventy-two years old. Harry died shortly before his eightieth birthday from a heart attack. Dad and Mom were at their bedsides, supporting them through these health crises until the end of their lives.

After I got my social work degree, Dad finally seemed able to admit to me that his relationship with his father Harry was filled with a tremendous amount of anxiety. It got so bad that once, while in a discussion with Harry, Dad actually passed out. He was so concerned about it that he went to a psychiatrist for help. Not only was he feeling very frightened and confused, he wanted to make sure he never reacted in the same way again. He didn't want his father to have that much control over his emotional state.

It was at this time that I began to see just how seriously broken the relationship between my father and grandfather had become. That fainting episode occurred when Dad initially began to face, and explore, the true nature of his relationship with his father. It was his first realization about how incredibly painful it was for him. That was when he began to openly speak with my mom about it too.

Over time, Dad slowly began to unveil other stories to us about things his parents had done to him and the damage they had caused. There was one story in particular he remained fixated on in his later years. He bitterly explained how when he was a soldier he sent fifty dollars a month from his army paychecks back home to his parents, with the understanding that Harry would put the money in a bank. He was supposed to save it for my dad, so that when he returned from the war, he'd have some money saved up as a cushion to help him get started in civilian life.

But when Dad came home from the army, he learned that Harry had taken his money and used it to pay for Edith's wedding. My dad was devastated by this news. I remember Dad telling me that he simply couldn't believe that while he was away risking his life, his father had just handed the money over to Edith.

In his eighties and nineties, Dad repeatedly returned to telling this story as a representation of the kind of man his father was. What Harry had done was the ultimate betrayal, Dad felt, and it was unforgivable. He literally took this anger to my grandfather's grave—in the sense that he made the deliberate decision not to visit the graves of his parents after their funerals. He saw this as his retribution for them not being emotionally available when he needed them the most.

Dad's relationships with his siblings were also very complicated. His stepbrother, Sidney, grew up to be an unstable adult. He lived in California, and we didn't see him very often. Sidney's early fondness for guns became a lifelong passion, which disturbed my dad, who vividly remembered what he had almost done to their brother, Jules. Uncle Sidney became a security guard, and Dad found that horrifying.

I remember as a child being on a family vacation at a dude ranch in Arizona. One day there was a knock on the door of our cabin. My dad opened the door, and there stood Sidney, dressed like a cowboy, from his hat to his boots, with a pair of six-shooters at his side. Sidney was a short man, but his getup made him look tall. He seemed like a real cowboy to Susie and me. He wasn't, but Dad immediately realized the *guns* were real and began chastising Sidney for having loaded weapons near our family. He demanded that he leave.

Yet, during the many periods when Uncle Sidney couldn't hold down a job, Dad sent him and his wife money to help them get by. He could not abandon him.

Dad's relationship with his brother Jules was by far the most challenging for him. Unlike Sidney, Jules had stayed in Chicago and he was at our house all the time. He believed appearances were very important—a very different value from Dad's—and he bought expensive cars, clothes, and jewelry to make it seem like he had a lot of money. He was supposed to be working with my dad at the scrap-metal business they had inherited from my grandfather, but, continuing his behavior from his earlier years, he rarely showed up for work—although he continued to collect his paycheck from Dad.

My dad would never admit it out loud, but on some level he truly valued his relationship with Jules. They became traveling companions after they were both widowed, and took many cruises together. They became companions in life as well. They understood each other. This created a sort of mutual comfort and shorthand in communication.

Despite longstanding issues about trust, the fact that they were brothers always trumped past disagreements or transgressions. Jules was still at our house a lot. They enjoyed sharing meals, watching TV, and sitting in the yard. When Jules got sick with a respiratory illness, it was my dad who was at his bedside, making decisions about his treatment and care. Jules's condition worsened, but he stubbornly refused to follow his doctors' recommendations. He was hospitalized for several days and ultimately died there with my dad at his side. This was in 1992, when my dad was seventy-five.

Jules was the only remaining member of Dad's original nuclear family. Although Dad never talked about it, it was clear that Jules's death was a significant loss for him. In addition, the close circle of friends that had been such a huge part of my parents' lives had fallen away due to death. It seemed to me that Dad became afraid to make any new, close friends for the remainder of his life because he was fearful he would lose them as well. It was an all-too-familiar pain he didn't want to experience again.

From the time we were little, Susie and I always knew that we would go to college someday. My parents emphasized the importance of a good education as being the only way to get a good job and build a career. I know that Dad felt so strongly about it because he himself didn't go to college. It was an opportunity he never had, growing up as he did during the Great Depression.

So when he talks about education in his autobiography, it's more about his high school years.

I am very good at school. I enter summer school to skip half a grade. I attend a four-year technical high school to learn electrical skills. I do not go to prom, because it is the Depression.

And he describes his first job while in high school:

After school I used to work at the Clark movie theatre as an usher. I got fired because I refused to hang signs after the theatre closed and I was off the clock. I never worked so hard for twenty-five cents an hour. I also sell shoes at Berland's women's shoe store at Wieboldt's department store. When the store closes, I put away stock without any extra pay, which is forty cents an hour plus a little extra money I make selling bows.

Dad's work ethic developed at a very young age. He strongly believed he should earn his own wages and contribute to his family, especially during the Great Depression. This ethic, along with his fiscal acumen, would serve him well throughout his life.

From the time my dad was a young boy, he was always

very good at mathematics, financially responsible, and a good businessman. Even at the age of twelve, he had a feeling there was going to be a huge financial collapse. He tried to talk to his father and begged him to take his money out of the bank. But Harry refused to listen. Undeterred, Dad went to the bank on his own and withdrew his life savings of thirteen dollars shortly before the country's economic collapse.

If you talk with people who lived through the Depression, most will tell you that it made a lifelong impression on them. One of the consequences for my dad was that he never trusted banks again. He'd keep money in multiple banks, in limited amounts, as his own personal safeguard.

When he was older and I would take him to do errands, as we drove around he would tell me, "I have money in that bank, and that one, and that one too." Playfully, I would call him the bankers' version of Johnny Appleseed, because he kept planting money—like seeds in these banks—and it would continue to grow. He always laughed, but would also warn me not to assume that another depression could not happen again, adding that it was "always a possibility." He made me promise I would never forget that and be wise with my financial affairs, just as he had been his whole life.

Along with Jules as a partner more or less in name only, Dad took over his father's scrap-metal business, Harry Sneider and Sons, when he was twenty-seven years old. I grew up hearing him call himself a junkman. It was backbreaking work. He got up at four in the morning to go to his warehouse to load up his truck. He'd return home around three in the afternoon, tired and dirty, moving slowly, speaking to us in short sentences.

The first thing he did upon entering the house was to take a shot of Canadian Club whiskey, and then he'd go take a shower. After that he would inevitably fall asleep in his La-Z-Boy chair. This was a great moment for Susie and me because it meant that the change in his pockets would fall out. What a treasure trove for us! We knew to look for the money quietly, because we were not to wake him up under any circumstance. When it was dinnertime, Mom would give us the signal, and *then* Susie and I could wake him up.

Once a year Dad would take Susie and me to his warehouse. It was a small, dirty building without windows. I remember there was an old, outdated calendar with bikini-clad pinup girls that hung on the wall, covered in dust and timelessly hanging on a nail. To Susie and me, the warehouse seemed like a magical place because our dad spent so much time there. Even at a young age we sensed the importance it had in his life and ours.

Many years later, as an adult, I talked to Dad about his job after he finally decided to give up the business. He was in his late seventies. By then I understood how physically demanding it had been and the sacrifices he made for our family. He provided a home and through his hard work offered a lifestyle that meant we never were hungry or lacked for anything we needed. I had some regret that as I was growing up I took this all for granted.

It was during this conversation that Dad admitted to me how much he hated the work his father had bequeathed to him. The early-morning awakenings were oppressive. Many times, the physical demands of the job felt overwhelming.

"Why did you keep on doing it, Dad, if it made you so unhappy?" I asked.

"It never occurred to me to stop," he replied simply. His most important goal, he explained, was to ensure that his children would have the opportunity to go to college and get a good education. This was something he never had in his life, and he had promised himself that he wanted to make this a reality for his offspring.

As Dad got older and older, I became concerned about how he was so focused on his distant past and how negative his memories were. I decided to try and shift his focus to the present. I talked to him about his children—my siblings and myself—and his grandchildren. I was happy to see his face brighten. "I'm a very lucky man," he said. "I have a wonderful family and I love them very much."

Gently, I told him that remaining bitter and angry at his father and brother, both long dead, prevented him from appreciating the good things he had in life, right here and now. I could see he was thinking about what I said. And then I realized there was another way to go about it, speaking in terms that would have a lot of resonance for him.

"Dad," I said, "you've gotten the best revenge of all. You're alive. You outlived them all. You have a good life with people you love, and who love you. We all happily take care of each other. They'd be jealous of the family you helped to create. Don't let past memories overwhelm you today."

"You know, I never thought about it like that before," Dad answered. "You're right." He laughed, and with a big smile on his face he told me, "I got the best revenge by building our family in spite of them all."

We had many similar conversations after that. When other family members would hear Dad's anger at his parents and siblings reemerge, they too would gently guide him back into the present. We all tried to help him refocus on the positive. He agreed to try, and we knew that was all we could ask of him.

I remember this time in Dad's life so clearly. He was ninety-six. I thought about all that he'd gone through in those many years and how it had helped shape the man he had become. The pain related to the lack of love he experienced growing up inspired him to become a more loving parent and grandparent.

He was willing to make many sacrifices so his children could feel loved, be given opportunities to get an education, and be self-sufficient. He wanted to offer us everything he never had. He was a self-made man, who had the confidence to educate and challenge himself to face the tasks that needed to be done along the way.

In spite of this troubled early history, Dad repeatedly gave his parents and siblings money, a home, and emotional support when they asked for it. His deep feelings regarding the importance of family remained strong. He instilled that into my siblings and me. He always opened our home and his heart to friends and other relatives who were in need.

The process of aging had taken a toll on my dad, as it does on everyone. His physical abilities and his brain function had eroded as his body neared a century of life. Somehow he did not let these losses depress or defeat him. His sense of humor and ability to laugh at himself and with those around him was a comfort to us all. Every time I saw him I would ask how he was, and he would always answer, "I'm doing as well as can be expected." That is really all any of us can ask in our lifetimes.

Coping with Grief and the Loss of Family

One of my observations about Dad was that his grief over the loss of his parents and siblings sometimes came out expressed as anger. Losing a family member with whom you had a tumultuous relationship can still evoke a grief reaction, or other, different, unexpected eruptions of feelings. In my dad's case, he focused on all the things he'd wanted but felt he never received from them.

Just as Dad did, many people experience a wide variety of emotions at the loss of a family member. These feelings can include sadness, shock, anger, relief, happiness, depression, anxiety, helplessness, an overwhelmed sensation, and/or fear. Not only can the intensity and range of emotions be influenced by the nature of your relationship with your loved one, it can also be affected by how they died. For example, some people react to a sudden death, such as one caused by a car accident or a murder, in a different way than they might to the loss of a loved one who had been seriously ill for many years. But they are both losses.

It doesn't matter what your age is when you lose a parent or other relative. It remains a loss or an absence in your life regardless of the relationship you had. Your life is forever changed. The process of *experiencing* and *adapting to* these emotions—whatever they may be—can help you grieve, heal, and eventually continue on with your life. At times, you may even feel almost crippled by your loss and find it difficult to imagine life returning to normal.

In these situations, "normal" will take on a new meaning. It's impossible to predict how long it will take you to go through your grieving process or precisely how this process will unfold. It's not useful or realistic to place expectations on yourself in terms of how long it takes to mourn the loss of someone who had a significant place in your heart and your life.

For some, grief feels like a series of distinct moments in which they experience a wild "roller coaster" of emotions. For others, grief can feel like they are living in a fog or simply going through the motions on a day-to-day basis, much like when you're driving and arrive at your destination without remembering how you got there.

In both my work and my personal life, I've found that some people may never fully get over the loss of a loved one. However, almost always the intensity of the grief does begin to lessen with time. Again, it can be a moment-by-moment or day-to-day process. Some days will be overwhelming and other days may even offer joyful experiences or feelings of relief. You might feel guilt for enjoying these moments for the first time after the loss of a family member or friend. It's not unusual and, in fact, is often a standard part of the grieving process.

People in mourning will frequently have trouble sleeping or lose their appetite. This in turn can result in lowered energy levels, tearful episodes, or an inability to have any joy in anything. There is a tendency for some people who are grieving to want to isolate themselves from others. These symptoms can all resemble those of depression. If they go on for an extended period of time or affect your ability to function in other relationships, at work, or in school, you may want to seek counseling—professional help to guide you through this difficult process.

How you experience grief can also be affected by whether or not you got to say good-bye to the person who has died. In Chapter 4, "Coping with Cancer," I describe how my family and I were able to have a final farewell with my mom before she died. It can be a very meaningful experience for both the person dying as well as for their loved ones.

In their book *Caring for Your Parents*, authors Hugh Delehanty and Elinor Ginzler describe the significance of these conversations:

> *Saying good-bye to a dying parent can be a literal moment, a bedside exchange that distills an entire relationship and that resonates in memory. Or it can be an accumulation of experiences and times together—even, simply, the acts of discussing and preparing for those last days well in advance.*

In whatever way it happens, being able to say good-bye represents a turning point for adult children.

People who want to have this time to say good-bye, but don't manage to get it, can have a sense of nonresolution or an unfulfilled need, which only intensifies the sense of loss and grief.

In my experience, I've come to see that we all have different types of coping skills, and sometimes even ones we may not be aware of. If you have experienced a death or loss in the past, you may have found that something you did, or someone you turned to, helped you get through it. When facing a new mourning process, remembering those past experiences may help you get through it a little more smoothly.

Most people find that holidays or special occasions like birthdays or anniversaries will trigger memories of their loved one. Sometimes you can be caught off guard when you hear a song or see someone who reminds you of the person you lost. These feelings can be very painful, especially if they occur soon after the death of a loved one. Generally with time the intensity of these episodes will diminish as well.

There are things you can do to help yourself work through the mourning process so that you can find ways to move on with your life. The American Psychological Association offers these steps or strategies as a means to begin to work through grief:

- Talk about the death of your loved one with friends and colleagues in order to understand what happened and remember your friend or family member. Denying the death is an easy way to isolate yourself, and will frustrate your support system in the process.

- Accept your feelings. People experience all kinds of emotions after the death of someone close. Sadness, anger, frustration, and even exhaustion are all normal.

- Take care of yourself and your family. Eating well, exercising, and getting plenty of rest help us get through each day and move forward.

- Reach out and help others dealing with the loss. Helping others has the added benefit of making you feel better as well.

- Sharing stories of the deceased can help everyone cope. Remember and celebrate the lives of your loved ones. Possibilities include donating to a favorite charity, framing photos of fun times, passing on a family name to a baby, or planting a garden in memory. What you choose is up to you, as long as it allows you to honor that unique relationship in a way that feels right to you.

We are each of us unique, and the way you grieve is individual and will be specific to who you are at that moment in time. Other factors—your faith, spirituality, beliefs as to what happens after death, previous experience with loss, your personality—govern how you cope with the days that follow the death of a family member. Be gentle and patient with yourself and others as this process unfolds. The passage of time will reveal strategies that work and others that don't. Allow yourself whatever time you need to begin to move forward.

Chapter 2

My Father Goes to War

Understanding and Coping with Memory Loss

My dad was a member of a group called "the Greatest Generation," a term coined by journalist Tom Brokaw. This generation of men and women lived through the Great Depression. During World War II, many went on to serve in the military, while others contributed to the war effort at home. My dad was a soldier. He was a patriot, extremely proud of his service to his country.

When Dad was a resident at an assisted-living facility, he participated in a wonderful project there. The staff brought in a writer with expertise in memoirs to help residents write short books about their most treasured memories. My dad chose to write about his experience as a soldier. At a special event hosted by the facility, Dad proudly presented his book and talked about this special time in his life.

Reminiscing about life histories through oral or written stories can be a powerful experience for the elderly. It can be a vehicle for others to express their respect and admiration as listeners and readers, as well as a meaningful bonding experience.

The telling of these stories can often facilitate memories in seniors, although sometimes they get caught up repeating sad or bittersweet memories that cause them to relive their anger or loss. Old memories are more deeply ingrained in the brain, and can be easier for elderly people to access. In the previous chapter I discussed how my family and I tried to gently change Dad's focus from the negative to a more positive perspective. You may want to try this with your elderly loved ones as well.

Much of my dad's autobiography focused on his experience during the war. He was twenty-four when he was drafted.

War breaks out in Europe and President Roosevelt passes the Selective Service Act. I draw the lucky number fifty-three and am inducted into the army on May 13, 1941. I am shipped to Camp Davis, North Carolina, for basic training. I take an aptitude test and get a high grade. This gives me the privilege of picking which branch of the service I wish to enter. I figure the safest one is the coast artillery and designate that.

We live in barracks that have a coal-burning stove. I am handpicked by the sergeant to shovel the coal. He thinks it is hard work, but he is wrong. I am used to hard work in my father's scrap-metal business. The sergeant asks, "How'd it go?" when I am done.

I reply, "Just another job." The next day I am promoted to corporal.

Over the years, Dad frequently reflected on this time in his life. After he came home, he became an active member of his local chapter of the Veterans of Foreign Wars. He regularly attended meetings and enjoyed the company of the other post members. While in his eighties, Dad was out in front of his local grocery store, collecting money on one of the VFW poppy fundraising days. The one request he made of me when we discussed his wishes regarding his funeral was to make sure he had a military funeral. He wanted members of his VFW chapter to present a flag and salute him for his service.

Dad told me that he went into the war fully understanding that he might not survive. "The difference between soldiers that survived and those that didn't," he'd say, "was simply good and bad luck."

It was clear to me that Dad felt a real connection with his fellow soldiers; he would refer to them as "the brothers" he served with. "We had a closeness," he would tell me, "that people who haven't served in the military could never understand."

In reading Dad's autobiography, I was surprised by how vividly he recalled his time in the military and its level of detail.

I am due to have a thirty-day furlough on December 8, 1941, instead the Japs bomb Pearl Harbor

*at Oahu. The next morning I am on a troop train
headed for San Francisco. I arrive Christmas 1941
and am shipped to a "staging area" located at Angel
Island. Next I am put on a troop ship called the
Maui headed for the Philippines.*

*They are playing what I call homesick music.
The ocean is beautiful with phosphorescent light.
Later on I discover that I lucked out. The American
Army surrendered the Philippines to the Japanese.
I could have been forced on a death march. Instead
my ship goes on to Oahu, arriving January 7,
1942. It is thirty days after the Japanese attacked
Pearl Harbor.*

*The whole fleet is devastated. I wonder how
did they know which hangers to hit and which
to omit, and why were planes lined up like sitting ducks? The island is beautiful, but the dev-
astation is horrendous. We have no air force. It is
my opinion that had the Japanese brought their
troops, they could have easily captured the island
of Oahu.*

When Dad would talk about his wartime experiences,
his memories were vivid and detailed. My siblings and I
were often amazed by it. When my brother, Danny, went on
a vacation to Hawaii, he visited Pearl Harbor to honor our
dad. Dad's descriptions of the area had been so accurate—
all the way down to street names!—that Danny actually
retraced Dad's steps and accidentally found himself in a
restricted military area at Pearl Harbor.

After he told the guard about our dad, and explained how he'd stumbled across the restricted area, the guard escorted him off the base without incident. Danny believes that it was due to their mutual respect for Dad's service as a soldier.

These clear, old recollections were a sharp contrast to Dad's short-term memory problems and other memory deficits later in life. One day I sat in on one of his speech therapy sessions. He and the therapist were constructing a

Melvin Sneider in his army uniform served in World War II for 4 years.

family tree together. Dad, ninety-six at the time, was able to remember the names of his four children. However, he could only recall the names of two of his six grandchildren, even with me giving clues—like, "It begins with an 'M'" or "She is Caryn's daughter"—to help him along the way.

I could see by the expression on Dad's face that he was trying as hard as he could to come up with the names. He knew they were in his brain. But he was simply unable to access the information he was seeking. I was impressed that he didn't seem to be frustrated by this obvious deficit. He just seemed reassured when I supplied the missing names.

The stories my dad shared about his experience in World War II reflected many mixed emotions. For one thing, he was shocked by some of the decisions he witnessed during his military service.

*I am issued World War I equipment. It consists
of a 37 mm gun and a water-cooled .50-caliber
machine gun. Both are totally obsolete. Our battery has a table of organization that needs filling
so I am promoted to sergeant and in one day I am
"Sergeant of the Guard," which means I have to
stay awake all night long to guard the American
prisoners. I am told if I let any one of them escape,
I will have to do their time.*

When I read this section about the antiquated equipment, I was utterly amazed. "What's your explanation for
that, Dad?" I asked.

"In my opinion, the military brass didn't really care
about that," Dad said, although he added that funding may
have been an issue. But his theory was that the government
"Just wanted to get as many soldiers on the battlefield as
possible." He went on to tell me he had no confidence that
his gun would work properly.

I was speechless, trying to imagine what it must have
been like for our soldiers to go into battle with weapons and
gear that were so out of date and problematic. The courage
of my dad and his "brothers" fighting for their country under
these circumstances really humbled me. I tried to balance
my feelings of admiration for the bravery of these military
personnel with my horror that the U.S. government would
put them in harm's way so ill-prepared.

It's impossible for me not to think about the wars in
Iraq and Afghanistan. Getting properly designed vehicles
to protect our troops from improvised explosive devices, as

well as supplying the needed amounts of protective gear such as bulletproof vests, is an ongoing problem. Disputes and Congressional hearings about funding for our military rage on. I am struck by how in some ways so little has changed since World War II.

My dad shared a story about being stationed in Hawaii. He was told to clean up garbage and cigarette butts in an area that had a large stockpile of materials, which were covered by a huge cloth tarp. He peeked under the tarp and was amazed to see many large containers of mustard gas. He realized that if his unit were to come under attack, these containers—located very near the living quarters of the troops—could be deadly for them all if they were ignited. As a low-ranking solider, he wasn't sure what to do about this realization.

Not long after this, a general came to visit Dad's unit. He came over to speak with my dad as he was working, and asked if there was anything he could do to help him. Dad quickly answered that he was very worried about the safety of his comrades due to the proximity of the mustard-gas containers. To Dad's surprise and relief, the general agreed with him, and promptly arranged for all the containers to be removed.

One of the things that surprised me most about the stories and memories my dad shared over the years was his recollections about a friend he made when he was in Hawaii. He fondly remembered numerous details.

I have made friends with a Filipino named Suelo
Lapino, who is practically a slave to the big companies

> *that govern this island. The big players here are Castle*
> *& Cooke, Matson, and Hawaiian Pineapple.*

I believe that one of the reasons Dad developed this kinship with Suelo was because he saw him working so hard for so little money. He felt that Suelo was being taken advantage of by these huge companies. Dad was always a champion of the underdog. And he even made a rather outrageous, "Robin Hood" sort of gesture on Suelo's behalf.

> *I commandeer a GI truck and driver to transport*
> *a load of stolen used lumber, which I give gratis to*
> *my friend Suelo. In gratitude he invites me to din-*
> *ner in Waimanalo where he lives. He has caught a*
> *delicacy, a live crab, which his wife cooks. The big*
> *companies own his house and store and everything*
> *including his wages. He is picking sugar cane for*
> *them. I bring groceries I have purchased for our*
> *wonderful dinner. We have a big feast.*

When I read this, I asked him, "Weren't you ever worried about getting caught taking these supplies?"

Dad just laughed. "Nobody kept close watch on these things," he replied, "and I was never afraid of being discovered." Together these two men found time to celebrate their friendship in the midst of mutual hardships. I think it gave them both an opportunity to forget their surroundings and not think about the future, but live in the moment—giving them both precious moments to laugh and enjoy each other's company.

Numerous reports have documented how warriors returning from various combat situations experience an emotional cost as well as a physical toll. My dad was no exception. He reached an emotional breaking point when he continued to lose his "brothers," who he repeatedly saw being sent off to their deaths.

> *I am losing all my friends in the service who are being shipped out and becoming a teaching "cadre." Out of sheer boredom I call up the captain and tell him I wish to join the next "task force." I have become like my Japanese enemy, a fatalist. The next thing I know I find myself on one of a dozen LSM's, which are small landing crafts used for an invasion. They consist of approximately 125 men and they're equipped with a special unloading ramp.*

He went on:

> *I am now with a new unit called Battery E, 867th AAA AW Battalion. The first two days we are all seasick, including the sailors. The food is wonderfully fresh. We eat eggs and bacon. I move to the fantail and throw up. I go down and eat again. I end up at the fantail again. After the second time I learn my lesson and quit.*

After I'd read this part, I asked, "What was your state of mind? How did you feel at that time?"

Dad paused, closed his eyes for a moment, and then

said, "At that point, I was so depressed seeing all my buddies leave that I didn't really care if I lived or died."

I am leaning over the railing. Lo and behold it is now dusk and I see an ominous black submarine break the surface of the water to recharge his batteries. I think to myself if that is a Japanese submarine we are all dead. Thank god it is an American ship and our protection.

The voyage was a long one, and Dad had lots of time to think about the decision he'd made to volunteer on this mission. He viewed the men he was fighting alongside as his beloved family. He felt protected and respected by them. This type of relationship was something he believed he never got at home from his own family.

After a very long voyage crossing thousands of miles we arrive at the Mariana Islands, which include Guam, Saipan, and Tinian. It is dusk, and I think I hear a thunderstorm. It appears in the distance that there is lightning and thunder.

When Dad finally arrived at his destination, he was shocked by what he found.

I discover that there has been shell fire from battleships that I cannot see. We land on Saipan at a town called Garapan. But there is no town. All I see are dead Japanese men scattered all around me.

*The marine infantry has done our job ahead of us.
I have the utmost respect for the marines. But they
paid a terrible price.*

*Livestock are running loose, including chick-
ens and a hog that was shot through the mouth.
We capture a dozen chickens and take the hog. I am
waiting for the chickens to lay eggs and nothing
happens. I ask a soldier we call "the hillbilly" why
they are not laying eggs. He tells me they are just
too scared. Instead we have chicken dinners.*

*My gun position consists of fifteen men, one
40 mm, and four .50-caliber machine guns on a
swivel stand tasked to guard Tanapag Harbor.
Later we are moved to Isley Field. Saipan is used
to launch one hundred B-29 bombers on a huge
raid over Japan. At the conclusion of the Battle for
Saipan, the 31,000 Japanese defenders had only
921 prisoners that remained.*

I believe it's important that those of us who have never
been a member of the military, and have never seen the
horrors that waging war elicits, should listen to those that
have. We ought to know how much the day-to-day life
in these situations changes them in unimaginable ways.
Like his comrades, my dad was forever changed by what
he witnessed as an army sergeant in World War II. He was
amazed that he survived and concluded that there must
have been a reason for that. He had to make some sense
out of his survival guilt. Dad decided the reason he lived
was that he was meant to go home and start a family. That

became his mission, his primary goal in life, after he left the service.

Understanding and Coping with Memory Loss

This chapter highlights the huge discrepancy between my dad's long-term memory and his short-term recall. This is a very common problem for the elderly. It's also a significant quality-of-life issue and can be a safety problem as well. What if a senior loved one forgets to turn off the stove when cooking?

With remarkable clarity, my elderly dad remembered small details from his life in the 1940s, but could not recall what he had just watched on TV or what he had for breakfast. He frequently lost his wallet, and would get frustrated and tell me, "I'm old and don't remember anymore." I heard a story about a woman whose father had the same problem so she bought several wallets and hid them all over his apartment so he always felt like he knew where it was.

If your parent is experiencing memory problems, there are some things you can do to help. The first step is to try and identify the exact nature of the problem before you explore the best ways to support her.

As we age, there is a normal degree of diminishment of brain function, which in turn affects our memory. There are different types of memory loss, and different causes for each. According to experts in this field, sometimes memory loss can be reversible. For example, a mild head trauma, a brain tumor, or improper medication use can cause memory loss, and all can be treated. It's important to see a doctor when memory loss suddenly occurs. Getting the right diagnosis as quickly as possible is key.

Dementia and Alzheimer's disease are terms that are often heard in reference to memory loss. The National Institutes of Health (NIH) defines dementia as "a loss of brain function that occurs with certain diseases. It affects memory, thinking, language, judgment, and behavior." These types of memory losses are very challenging because there is no understanding about what to do when you can't remember something. "Most types of dementia are nonreversible (degenerative). Nonreversible means the changes in the brain that are causing the dementia cannot be stopped or turned back."

The NIH goes on to say: "Alzheimer's disease is the most common type of dementia. Lewy body disease is a leading cause of dementia in elderly adults. People with this condition have abnormal protein structures in certain areas of the brain."

Studies now show that the part of the brain that sorts through information begins to decline during the aging process. People who continually use certain skills, like regularly speaking in a foreign language, may find that those skills are not as diminished with aging. As I mentioned earlier, old information that is well known to the senior also tends to remain more intact.

It can sometimes be tricky to detect signs that there

are memory problems. People can be adept at hiding their deficits. If you're not around an elderly loved one on a regular basis for long periods of time, it can be missed. According to gerontologist Cheryl Kuba in her book *Navigating the Journey of Aging Parents*, there are signals to watch for that can indicate the presence of Alzheimer's disease. They include:

- Recent memory loss that affects job skills

- Difficulty performing familiar tasks

- Problems with finding the right words

- Disorientation of time and place

- Poor or decreased judgment

- Problems with abstract thinking

- Misplacing things

- Changes in mood or behavior

- Changes in personality

- Loss of initiative

By the way, Alzheimer's disease is not just something that afflicts the elderly. People in their forties or fifties can begin to demonstrate these symptoms. These cases are known as early-onset Alzheimer's disease, and this is especially devastating for people who are still working and may be the primary source of income for their families. This illness directly affects their ability to parent, and relationships with their spouses are severely tested. Because of their relatively young age, friends, colleagues, and family members may not recognize these symptoms for what they are and misunderstand why these symptoms are occurring. Conflicts can arise, causing tension, job loss, or the severing of longstanding relationships.

Here are some things to do—recommended by the Mayo Clinic—that can help slow down loss of memory, regardless of one's age.

Stay mentally active

Just as physical activity helps keep your body in shape, mentally stimulating activities help keep your brain in shape—and might help keep memory loss at bay. Do crossword puzzles. Read a section of the newspaper you normally skip. Take alternate routes when driving.

Socialize regularly

Social interaction helps ward off depression and stress, both of which can contribute to memory loss. Look for opportunities to get together with loved ones, friends, and others—especially if you live alone.

Get organized

You're more likely to forget things if your home is cluttered and your notes are in disarray. Jot down tasks, appointments, and other events in a special notebook, calendar, or electronic planner.

Sleep well

Sleep plays an important role in helping you consolidate your memories, so you can recall them down the road. Make getting enough sleep a priority.

Eat a healthy diet

A healthy diet might be as good for your brain as it is for your heart. Eat fruits, vegetables, and whole grains. Choose low-fat protein sources such as fish, lean meat, and skinless poultry. What you drink counts, too. Not enough water or too much alcohol can lead to confusion and memory loss.

Include physical activity in your daily routine

Physical activity increases blood flow to your whole body, including your brain. This might help keep your memory sharp.

Manage chronic conditions

Follow your doctor's treatment recommendations for any chronic conditions, such as depression, or kidney or thyroid problems. The better you take care of yourself, the better your memory is likely to be.

If your senior loved one is experiencing memory problems, having him see a gerontologist—a specialist who deals with the issues and problems of aging—is a good option if it's at all possible. He or she can order psychological testing, brain scanning, and a psychosocial history to be performed if indicated. The psychosocial history looks at various aspects of a person's life, such as family history, work, education, and support network. It helps the evaluator to have this in-depth assessment to gain more insight into how the patient is functioning.

Laboratory or blood-work testing may also be required to get a comprehensive picture of the day-to-day functioning of the senior. It can be enormously valuable to ensure that a relative or close friend goes to these appointments, so that they can help provide accurate information and observations to the physician. I also suggest bringing along pen and paper or an iPad or tape recorder, in order to record information discussed in your visit.

You can expect the physician to ask numerous questions in order to formulate a correct diagnosis. The Mayo Clinic shares a list that can help you and your senior come to the appointment better prepared:

• How long have you been experiencing memory problems?

- What medications—including prescription drugs, over-the-counter drugs, and dietary supplements—do you take regularly? What is the dosage of each?

- Have you recently started a new drug? What tasks do you find too difficult to perform or finish?

- What have you done to cope with memory problems? Have these things helped you?

- Do you drink alcohol? How much do you drink daily?

- Have you recently been in an accident, fallen, or injured your head?

- Have you recently been sick?

- Have you recently felt sad, depressed, or anxious?

- Have you recently experienced a major loss, change, or stressful event in your life?

- What is your daily routine? How has your routine changed recently?

Earlier in this chapter I mentioned that there are things you can do on a day-to-day basis to help your senior who is experiencing memory loss. I described how I sat in on a speech therapy session with my dad. Not only did he have difficulty remembering the names of his grandchildren, he also had trouble coming up with names of different animals. When the speech therapist created categories, like "farm animals," "pets," and "zoo animals," Dad was then able to list numerous animals in each category. The therapist explained that creating categories helps seniors with memory problems focus more carefully and better access information. For example, when thinking about groceries to buy, grouping similar items can be helpful; if he wants juice, milk, eggs, and bacon, he could reinforce this by categorizing it as drinks and breakfast items.

A calendar can be a simple but very effective tool. Encourage your elderly loved one to write down appointments, meetings, get-togethers, birthdays, anniversaries, and so on. Make sure it's in a place that's easily visible in an area that is seen and accessed daily.

Does your senior have photographs of family members or friends? Putting their names on the photographs can be helpful to stimulate memory. Also, if the senior is in a nursing home or assisted-living facility, staff members can reference these photos and further engage your loved one in conversation. Especially if it's done consistently, it encourages ongoing dialogue between the staff and the senior, as well as helping to support his memory.

Take a look around your senior's living space. Is it messy or cluttered? Try to organize things and minimize clutter. At the same time, do keep items in their regular spots. It really can help someone with memory issues if frequently used items, like glasses, medications, or hearing aids, have a specific place where they're consistently kept.

Darby Morhardt, MSW, LCSW, PhD, has been working with Alzheimer's patients and their families for over twenty-five years. She is a research associate professor at Northwestern University Feinberg School of Medicine's Cognitive Neurology and Alzheimer's Disease Center. She offers insights about how to continue to nurture and build relationships with people who have memory loss.

"The best thing you can do for a person with dementia is recognition of the person they were and are and be compassionate in your communication," she says. "Always remember to help the person with the illness 'save face.' If the person thinks they are in a different city and it really makes no difference that they are told otherwise, it is best to not correct, but to connect on an emotional level."

This is solid advice. Really be selective about when you attempt to correct your elderly loved ones when they are confused about a particular subject. Trying to convince them they are wrong can cause an unwanted emotional battle and can also highlight their deficits which can create an array of negative feelings for all concerned.

Anyone who has been a caregiver for a person with memory problems understands that there are moments of anger and frustration for both parties. It can be painful if you're the caregiver who's just attempting to help your loved one, and to receive verbal (or even physical) abuse in return. It's natural to take it personally. You might end up feeling very hurt, confused, or unappreciated.

"Spouses and adult children can be confused by the behavior of someone with dementia," says Morhardt, "and think that what they are doing and saying is purposefully hurtful. It is important to recognize that it is the disease talking."

Remember that people with dementia or other types of memory problems do not have the ability to control their emotions. They don't understand how to correct the limitations presented by their illness. If you find yourself as a caretaker feeling more depressed, anxious, short-tempered, and/or emotionally and physically drained, these are signals that you need to take a break.

Make arrangements for another caretaker to step in. There may be a time when you need to consider a program like assisted living or a nursing home that can offer twenty-four-hour support. (You can learn more about nursing homes in Chapter 11.) Finally, if there *are* moments of clarity with your loved one, allow yourself to relish them. They can offer a real sense of comfort and connection for you both.

Chapter 3

Marriage, Home, and Family

*Adult Children as Caretakers and
the Challenges of Long Distance*

When my dad returned from the war, he wanted to get
a home of his own as quickly as possible. Although
he was able to find employment working in his father Harry's scrap-metal business, he was eager to be on his own. He
held tightly to the powerful resentment he felt toward his
father for taking his money and giving it to his sister.

So he found a small, inexpensive apartment in a residential hotel called the Uptown Granada, located in a
modest neighborhood in Chicago with an elevated train
nearby that offered a cheap way to commute around the
city. To save money, Dad shared his little apartment.

Dad was in search of a woman to marry, and thanks to
the Uptown Granada, he got lucky and didn't have to look

far. The Granada had a telephone switchboard, and soon Dad took notice of a young woman who worked there. Her name was Beverly Elaine Felkoff.

Dad began spending more time at that switchboard, talking and flirting with Beverly. She was pretty and intelligent. She was friendly and nice. He noticed she was a hard worker, too. These were qualities he believed were necessary in a life partner.

He wasn't interested in dating a lot of women. He didn't have the time, the disposition, or the inclination to do that. He was looking for a more serious woman, not a party girl. It never occurred to him to ask Beverly her age. She seemed mature and responsible. They began dating shortly after he noticed her.

When Beverly was sixteen, her father had died of high blood pressure. Her mother never really got over his death; she was unable to cope and get a job. It was up to Beverly to earn some income so that her family would survive.

Beverly was lucky to have gotten her switchboard job. It was steady employment, with regular hours. She could help her family because of it. And it gave her a chance to get out of their apartment. She wanted to be with other people and have a social life.

My dad would find out much later that Beverly was just seventeen when they started dating. He was twenty-nine at the time. Dad would later tell us that he'd always assumed she was much older because of the way she carried herself and the responsibilities she'd been forced to take on at such a young age. In reality the age difference didn't really matter much to either of them. My dad got up the nerve to propose a couple of years after they started dating. To my dad's joy, Beverly said yes.

The young couple didn't have much money between them when they got married. My dad was working long hours alongside his father. It was difficult, tedious work, but Dad was willing to do whatever he needed to create financial security for his wife and the children he hoped would soon come along.

They moved to an apartment building in Albany Park, a neighborhood where my mom's cousins lived. They were more like siblings to her, and they all shared a very close relationship. They spent a lot of time together, and Dad enjoyed socializing with them too. They had a lot in common. They shared similar interests and were all trying to save money to buy a house and begin their families. They hoped to get their fair share of the American Dream.

In addition to her warmly welcoming cousins and other family members, Dad became a part of Mom's circle of friends. These relationships were strong and meaningful for them both. Over the years my dad began to see the value of these relationships. He'd never really had long-term friendships before. It was a new experience for him, feeling supported and valued by family and friends. In turn, Dad was a loyal and constant friend to them as well.

My mom and my dad had very different kinds of personalities. Mom was very outgoing; she enjoyed socializing and meeting new people. She loved to talk and was a very engaging person. She dressed as stylishly as she could with the money she had. People just loved to be around her.

Dad, on the other hand, was a quiet man who preferred

listening to talking. He was not
interested in clothes or fashion,
but he did enjoy it when my mom
did what she could to dress up.

After a few years of marriage,
during which they lived very fru-
gally and saved their money, they
decided it was time to get their
own home. They chose a suburb
called Skokie, located north of
Chicago. It was a middle-class
area where new stores, good
restaurants, and good schools
were being built to meet the
needs of the quickly growing
young population.

*Melvin and his wife, Beverly,
after they were married in 1949.*

My parents decided to have their new house built for
them. They wanted a five-bedroom ranch-style home with
a spacious basement. It was going to cost $35,000, which
was a lot of money at the time. As time went on Dad had
several disagreements with the builder and didn't trust him
to complete the job as he had promised—leaving them
with a huge unfinished basement area.

So Dad decided to do all the work on the basement
himself. He had no experience with plumbing or wood-
work, but that didn't matter to him. He trusted his abilities
in mathematics. He also had confidence that if he found the
right books, he could learn what he needed to create a beautiful basement, completing his dream house. He was right.

When he was done, they had a basement complete with

two bedrooms, a bathroom, and a large family room, as well as a workshop filled with his tools. He knew he wanted to continue to work on home-improvement projects, and he did. Later in life, looking back at this time in Skokie, he would comment on how he taught himself all of these skills. Dad was rightfully proud of this achievement.

My parents moved into their new home in May of 1954. At the time, my mom was four months' pregnant with me. She would soon be put on bed rest. She'd had a couple of miscarriages before she had me. During this time in their new house, she was the perfect patient, not wanting to do anything to compromise this pregnancy. My dad continued to work his grueling schedule, getting up at four in the morning.

After my birth later that year, Mom would have more miscarriages. It was a joyful day when my sister Susie was born in August 1956. Dad was thrilled to have two girls, but he also hoped one day to have a son. He understood, though, that with the health issues associated with my mom's pregnancies, a son might not be a possibility.

My parents had moved to Skokie at just the right time. Our neighborhood was filled with families, with lots of children the same age as my sister and me. And Mom and Dad made many close friends who had similar lifestyles and backgrounds.

It was an ideal childhood. Susie and I would meet our friends at school, and afterward we'd wander around the neighborhood playing together. I barely remember seeing a grown-up. We all knew that when it started getting dark it was time to leave. Occasionally my mom would stand on the front porch and holler for us to come home. Dad used to say that her voice was "piercing." It was very loud and carried clearly down the block. It was much more effective than a bell.

I vividly remember the thick, green shag carpeting in our family room, where not just family but friends often hung out. That carpet was impossible to clean. Dad proudly put the new color television he bought in 1957 in the family room. It was the first color TV we'd ever seen. There were four stations to choose from. The picture at times became fuzzy and multiple lines would appear on the screen and jiggle. We didn't care.

All the TV stations would end their programming at night after the Johnny Carson show or a movie. They'd play "The Star-Spangled Banner," "America the Beautiful," or other patriotic music, and sometimes show the American flag. Then the screen would just display a black-and-white picture of a test pattern.

Eventually our fascination with television grew. A newer, smaller color TV was purchased and placed in my parents' bedroom. We'd gather there on their bed to watch *Bonanza*. Another favorite show that my parents watched with us was *Walt Disney's Wonderful World of Color*. Walt Disney himself would host the show and introduce the various segments. I remember how lucky we'd feel when they'd air a Disney film like *The Parent Trap* or *Dumbo*.

In the early 1960s my dad decided to build a new addition onto our house. He'd made a nice sum in the stock market on a company called Fairchild Camera and Instrument. He wanted to have a family room (which would later sport that green shag rug) and attach a garage to the house. The contractor asked Dad if he wanted to install a bomb shelter in the backyard as well, since the hole they needed to dig for the garage and the family room was very deep.

This was around the time of the Cuban Missile Crisis, when it felt like the world was on the brink of a nuclear war. Tensions were running high between the United States and Russia.

Having lived through World War II, Dad believed it was always possible the United States would face another war. He believed having the bomb shelter was a good idea. He wasn't alone in this. Building bomb shelters was a very popular trend in the 1960s. The memory of Hiroshima was still fresh in the minds of many Americans, including my dad. They wanted to have a safe place for their family to go quickly if there was ever a nuclear attack.

Our bomb shelter had one large room for sleeping, with four foldaway beds. It also had a second room, a kitchen area with a sink and stove, where food and water were stored. There was also an enclosed bathroom space, which had a toilet with a large pail in it. There was no running water, of course, but it had electricity. The whole thing was constructed well below ground, with steel and concrete reinforcements. And it had an escape tunnel that led to a hatch popping out of the back patio.

Friends and neighbors asked about reserving space if there was a nuclear attack or other unexpected emergency. That was the adult perspective. For us kids, it was simply a wonderful place to play hide-and-seek.

In 1966 my parents attended a funeral that would ultimately change our lives forever. A woman who was a third cousin of Dad's had died of cancer. When Dad

Caryn, Susie, Beverly, Melvin, Iris and Danny after Caryn and Danny's adoption in 1966.

and Mom got to the funeral home, they overheard other relatives arguing.

The woman who had died left behind a thirteen-year-old son, Danny, and a seventeen-year-old daughter, Caryn. Their father had walked out and left them while their mother was sick with cancer.

The relatives were arguing about who was going to be responsible for them. Some were willing to consider taking Danny but not Caryn. My parents were appalled to witness a scene like that, before their mother was even buried. And they both felt strongly that these siblings had been through enough and should not be separated, especially under these circumstances.

When they got home, Mom said to Dad, "Let's adopt them."

My dad quickly agreed.

They then called Susie and me together for a family

meeting. I was twelve and Susie was ten. Mom asked, "How would you feel about having a new brother and sister?"

I wondered how she knew the sexes of the babies she must be carrying. So I asked her about it. She and my dad carefully explained what they had witnessed at the funeral home. They told us the story of how Caryn and Danny had lost their parents, and asked if we would be willing to bring them into our home as part of our family.

My initial reaction was to think how fun it would be to have an older sister and a brother. I also realized this was a chance for Dad to have the son he had wanted. Susie expressed no reservations. It never occurred to us what an incredible undertaking this would be for my dad and mom; they'd be parenting two kids who had become orphaned under very traumatic and tragic circumstances.

The four of us were unanimous: we wanted to bring Caryn and Danny into our home and our lives if they were willing to do it.

Their aunt brought them to our house for an awkward initial visit. This was unfamiliar terrain for all of us. None of us kids knew what to say to each other or how to act. All four of us were quiet.

It didn't occur to me at the time that Danny and Caryn really had no other, better options available to them. The day they officially moved in was awkward for us kids. None of us could know what the future would hold. It was sort of like an arranged marriage.

Caryn and Danny were nervous, quiet, polite, and shy. Susie and I were uncertain about what to say or do. Then Mom stepped into the breach. In the days that followed, she tactfully gave us all cues about what to do and where to go.

Danny later told me that for months afterward, he'd stare out his bedroom window, waiting to see if his father would come to get him.

In later years, both Danny and Caryn talked about the tenderness and patience of my parents during those difficult early months. Mom was especially sensitive and tried to anticipate their needs. She created an atmosphere in which they could talk frankly about what they were feeling.

It naturally took some time for them to feel comfortable. They found themselves in a new situation, although one immediate positive was freedom from the financial constraints that had become a regular part of their lives. I remember Danny opening our big fridge full of food and just staring at it in amazement. He would ask Mom if he could get something to eat. She'd gently remind him that this was now his home. He could take whatever he wanted to eat without asking permission.

My dad would have told you he was one of the luckiest people on Earth because of his children. I often heard him tell people how proud he felt about the family he created. And we all agreed how incredibly enriched our lives were when our family expanded this way.

In less than a year after they moved in with us, Danny and Caryn began referring to our parents as "Mom and Dad."

Caryn went on to college at Miami of Ohio and later went to Washington University. While in St. Louis she worked at a local television station, and after graduating she went into television production, formed her own production company, and continues to make television shows here and for the BBC in London. Among her proudest achievements are *Roseanne* and *The Cosby Show*—both groundbreaking and influential.

Danny went to the University of Iowa. In thinking about a career, he always knew he didn't want to sit behind a desk from nine to five. He'd spent time working with Dad in his warehouse, but he found the work and the long hours grueling. Dad had planned to give the business to him. However, Danny frankly explained to him that he didn't think he could do the work. He was afraid of disappointing him by not continuing Harry Sneider and Sons. Much to Danny's relief, Dad didn't challenge his decision. He wanted a better life for him. He told him he understood and he genuinely did.

My brother initially sold Grolier educational books and realized he needed, he said, "a hook to get people interested." So he taught himself magic and convinced a local school to let him do a magic show. He incorporated humanistic values and lessons into his show. For example, he liked to use the magic phrase "I am special" as a part of his show. He wanted to teach kids about how important self-esteem is.

Danny's magic performances became so successful that eventually he stopped selling the books. He created an act under the stage name "Magic Dan" and today is well known in San Francisco and around the West Coast. He also does charity shows for the elderly, sick children, and people suffering from AIDS.

Susie went into a teaching career, working with special-needs students. She's been teaching for over thirty years. She won an award as one of the best teachers of the year.

I got a social work degree and spent many years working as a medical social worker. I covered the emergency room and a cancer unit, as well as doing a long stint on a rehabilitation unit with patients who had catastrophic medical problems such as strokes, burns, amputations, head injuries, and serious neurological problems. I did a lot of individual, family, and group counseling with my patients and families. I also helped set up their transitions from the hospital.

I began a writing career after my daughter Grace was born. I wrote an award-winning book to help people struggling with infertility, and continue to write health-related articles with an informative and advocacy theme.

My mom felt that volunteering for a worthy cause was important. She devoted herself to the Children's Asthma Research Institute and Hospital, located in Denver, Colorado. She believed asthma was a frightening and potentially deadly illness affecting children. She was willing to travel to Denver, which was where the heart of the research and the leading hospital was located.

She was a local fundraising leader in our town and deeply involved in the organization. She'd fly out to Denver to meet the kids and visit the staff at the hospital. And she took us there to meet them, too. She wanted us to see why she did this work and why it was so important to her.

My mom had other enthusiasms as well. She loved to go shopping at the Old Orchard Shopping Center in Skokie. Pretty much every day she went there with her girlfriends. They took delight in the "shopping hunt" and the thrill of finding bargains. My dad was always baffled at these shopping expeditions, their frequency, and why my mother would want to spend her time and his money in that way. But I think he understood there was an important social component to it.

Another unfortunate passion of my mother's was smoking cigarettes. She smoked about three packs of Silva Thins a day. She would send us kids to the corner store to replenish her supply when she was running low. The guy at the store knew us very well because we were there so often.

When I was a teenager, research began to emerge about the dangers of smoking too much. Dad referred to her cigarettes as "coffin nails," making it clear he disapproved of her unhealthy habit and the coughing attacks it would trigger. In fact, we all begged her to stop smoking. We even put antismoking literature on her pillow, hoping that would get her to stop or at least reduce the number of cigarettes she smoked. One time we even hid her cigarettes. She became so furious she told us we'd better return the cigarettes immediately or we would be out the door.

Dad loved to smoke pipes. When we were growing up, our house was filled with a blend of pipe and cigarette smoke. But when Dad saw what the cigarette smoking was doing to Mom, with her increasingly frequent coughing, he quit smoking his pipes permanently. And he continued to try to get Mom to stop smoking. But he was no more successful than we kids were.

Another passion of Mom's was her pride in her fingernails. They were, in a way, her trademark. People often commented on them. They were very long and always immaculately groomed and polished. She spent hours on her nails every day, sometimes tending to them until one or two in the morning. This was another pastime my dad had little patience or understanding for.

Our friends loved to come and hang out at our house. They viewed Dad as a fair man, and they could joke with him. They knew what to expect from him. And he welcomed them into our home. My mother was a magnet for our friends. They'd come gather around our kitchen table and talk with her.

She loved to hold court, surrounded by the cloud of her cigarette smoke. She was a great talker, but she was also a great listener, and she had a wonderful sense of humor. Our friends would eagerly tell her their problems or talk about what was going on in their lives. She would offer sage advice. It always amazed me how my friends would talk so openly to my mom about intimate things, about what they were thinking or feeling. It was clear to me how comfortable they were around her.

Adult Children as Caretakers and the Challenges of Long Distance

In recent years, thanks to improvements in medical research, better medications, more effective treatment, wider availability of information on good dieting, and more proactive health measures, people are living longer. And as I touched on in the introduction, our parents are living longer. This means that those of us who are their adult children may also be taking on additional caretaking responsibilities, a situation that can be especially challenging for those who don't live in close proximity to their parents. It requires good communication and close collaboration with your siblings—if you have them—and/or other designated caretakers. This is so important in identifying what help is needed and who will be the person to offer the necessary support services.

It's important to keep in mind that past relationships you had with siblings or other family members directly influence your ability to assume a caretaker role today. You may have family scattered in different states or other countries. There may be a sibling or close relative who lives close to your aging parents but is unable or unwilling to take on the caretaker role.

I encourage you to take some time to reflect on your relationships with your siblings or other close relatives who might be a member of the caretaking team. Here are some questions you may find useful in thinking about this:

- How well did you and your siblings/relatives get along as you were growing up? Whom did you have fights with?

- Did you eventually resolve these conflicts, or are there still unsettled issues that have created ongoing turmoil in your relationships as adults? For example, was one child labeled the "troublemaker," and another the "good kid"? What labels, if any, did you grow up with? Do you feel they're applicable now?

- How often are you in contact with your siblings?

- Do you have the kind of relationship in which you can have a candid exchange of ideas and opinions without any residual resentment?

- What kinds of relationships did your parents have with their parents, siblings, and other family members?

As you explore the answers to these questions, a blueprint will likely emerge for you about how your current familial relationships have been shaped. And these answers can help influence how you approach your role as a potential caretaker.

Regardless of the current health of your elderly loved ones, try to spend some time thinking about what type of assistance you'd be willing and able to offer them if they were unable to take care of themselves. Keep in mind that many challenges and obstacles can arise. These considerations include:

- It can be difficult to maintain a balance between taking care of your parents, your work, and your commitment to your immediate family.

- Different careers create different demands in terms of time, stress, and travel.

- There can be a barrier created by sibling/ family relationships, labels, and dynamics that remain in place after childhood.
- You may have issues in your personal life to deal with, such as relationship problems, financial problems, or time pressures.

- You and your siblings may have made very different choices about where you decided to live and build your life. Distance is a key factor when considering the caretaker role.

- Your individual relationship with your parents is unique to you and may differ greatly from that of your siblings and other family members.

- Your current relationship with your parents was greatly influenced by the parenting messages they gave you when you were growing up. For example, if you grew up in an abusive home, there's a good chance you'll feel less inclined to help your parents in later life than would someone who grew up in a loving home, with parents modeling the importance of familial relationships.

Developing insight and awareness of these issues can be extraordinarily useful. It can help you, your siblings, or other involved relatives create a more effective caretaking team.

As you explore the answers to the questions posed on these pages, I hope that a helpful understanding will emerge for you about how your current relationships have been shaped—one that will help you thoughtfully approach your potential role as a caretaker for the senior loved ones in your life.

With that in mind, here are some key starting points to help lay some groundwork *before* they become ill or disabled:

- Have an honest talk together. Encourage them to discuss their fears about their future aging. What type of help they would want, for example, if they had no mobility and couldn't prepare their own meals or take care of their personal needs? You don't want to wait until there's an emergency—a health or financial crisis—to start considering these important scenarios. You need time to consider these issues and begin the proper planning.

- Ask your parents, "What do you need from us to help you continue to live well at this particular time of your life?" Continue to raise these questions with them as they grow older and their health, finances, or other circumstances change.

- Identify who would be willing to help them. Get specific names of family members and/ or friends. Or would they prefer professional assistance, if finances permit this?

- Would they consider leaving their home in order to receive a higher level of care, such as assisted living, or are they committed/determined to stay at home, no matter what happens with their health and/or finances?

- Include all siblings and relevant family/friends in this discussion, whether it's in person, by Skype, via FaceTime, or by telephone. This ensures that everyone has input and hears directly from your parents what their personal wishes are. Ideally, nothing that is said will then be subject to misinterpretation. Have a designated person take notes or record this important meeting and its contents for potential future reference for all concerned. Share copies of this information.

- Familiarize yourselves with your parents' financial situation, insurance coverage, and other resources. If the time comes that they require additional help, you'll know what kind of support is available. This kind of fact-finding will also highlight where potential gaps in service might be.

Once you've done all this, an important next step is to have all the siblings get together, whether in person, by Skype, or by phone. If you are an only child, are there other trusted family members or friends who can be involved? Have a candid discussion based on the information you've gathered. Here are some of the issues that should be explored:

- Do you need to make a list of specific areas where your parents need help at this time?

- When defining caretaker roles, closely explore all the available sibling/family/friend skills. For example, who lives close by, who has more financial resources, who understands health or insurance issues, who has more free time, who can offer in-person or driving assistance?

- Estimate the necessary frequency of the identified tasks. For example: daily bathing assistance or going on a weekly shopping trip for groceries and other household goods.

- Discuss who is available to help with these tasks. If there is a gap that you can't seem to cover, consider using outside help. Perhaps a friend, neighbor, or paid professional can be brought in to assist.

As I mentioned earlier, this role reversal, in which we take care of our parents instead of the other way around, can be emotionally difficult and stressful for all concerned. It can test everyone's patience and commitment.

Tensions often arise when a sibling or relative feels she's doing more than her share, or when parents or siblings don't do what they said they would. When people lose their independence, they can become angry and frustrated. On occasion these feelings may be directed at those who are trying to help them the most.

When these angry feelings are directed at you, it's important to remember that the source of the anger may not be you; rather, it could well be that it's the *circumstances* which are causing your parent to feel overwhelmed. If possible, try to communicate in new and meaningful ways by expressing your empathy and understanding. As difficult as this time can be, it can also be an opportunity for you to mend old misunderstandings.

Here are some additional suggestions that may be useful to you as you proceed through this planning process:

- Be fair and flexible when dividing caretaker responsibilities. Know you may need to make adjustments as conditions change.

- Be respectful of each other and maintain your parents' dignity as much as possible.

- Plan a follow-up session in an agreed-upon time frame, and encourage everyone to participate so that close communication is maintained.

- For members of the caretaking team who

don't live close by, maybe they can help
with insurance or phone calls or other tasks.
Perhaps they can plan periodic visits in order
to give others a much-needed break.

- Those who can't assist in person may be able
  to offer financial support.

- If more assistance is needed, perhaps
  spouses, other relatives, or friends/neighbors
  can be recruited to help.

- It may be useful to consult your local
  senior center to find a social worker or a
  resource person/agency specializing in home
  support for the elderly. Utilize other skilled
  professionals if more help is needed or
  conditions deteriorate.

- All caretakers need a break at some point. If
  you find yourself feeling highly stressed or
  overwhelmed, be sure to allow yourself this
  time. It will reenergize you. This ultimately
  helps all involved. The team should recognize that the primary caretaker is going to
  need support.

- Local hospitals with geriatric programs
  usually have social workers who can provide
  useful information. They may be able to

point you to programs that offer care and
assistance for seniors.

• Your physician can also be a good resource for
information on appropriate care opportunities.

Are you geographically distant from your elderly loved
one? You can still contribute to his well-being in a variety
of ways. A good place to start is to familiarize yourself with
the medical diagnosis that's been given to him. Do some
research by speaking with a doctor or trusted friend, or by
visiting well-established websites, to gather all the information you can about the medical problem. What are your
parent's symptoms, and what is the prognosis? What treatment options are available, and which are recommended by
a reliable health professional? This research will help you
get a better understanding of the type of caretaker support
that will be needed, what the necessary components are,
and how long it might be necessary.

Another critical task is to collect all the medical bills
and insurance information so that you know what is being
covered. Look for potential gaps in coverage and identify
where additional financing may be needed. Create a filing
system to keep track of all the paperwork you will inevitably
receive. While going through this material, put together a
resource and contact list that you can share with other caretakers. It can save a lot of time and anxiety for all concerned
when a problem develops. With this in place, you immediately know whom to contact and how to reach them.

This contact list should include family caretaker names

and phone numbers. In addition, do include the names, addresses, and phone numbers for your parent's local hospital, physicians, and home health-care staff, as well as the director of the health-care program and the manager in charge of the staff.

If your loved one is in a nursing home or assisted-living program, include the main phone number, address, and the name and number of the person in charge of the facility. If there's someone else you need to contact with questions or staff concerns, include him or her, too.

Establishing the Caregiver Plan, and Finding the Right Caregiver

Earlier in this chapter, I suggested that you and other members of the caretaking team set up a meeting so that you could establish a solid caregiver plan. I recommended a follow-up meeting as well. Utilize these meetings to analyze what's been accomplished and also to identify problem areas. Take some time to evaluate who's been doing what. Depending on the setting, physicians, nurses, companions, or other home health-care staff can also be participants in this meeting. Their input can be invaluable; their professional experience can lead them to offer good insights, especially in areas you may have overlooked or misunderstood.

It has been my personal experience that finding the right caretaker can be extremely challenging. Sometimes having the wrong caretaker can add more anxiety to an already-fraught situation. It can be especially difficult to be at a distance when you don't have confidence that the person taking care of your loved one is competent and compassionate.

One day in 2014, Susie and I had taken a break and gone to a movie theater. The trailers had just begun when I got a phone call from our brother, Danny, in California. He told me that Dad's home health aide had called him in a panic when Dad accidentally pulled out his catheter. He had just been discharged from the hospital less than a day earlier. The caretaker had forgotten how to reach Susie and me, who were only ten minutes away. We were the first ones to call in an emergency.

It was impossible to trust this aide again after going through that. It also created doubts about the agency we were using. We began to question the agency's ability to accurately assess their staff and their qualifications. Ultimately, we felt we had to ask the aide to leave, and Susie and I stayed with Dad and took care of him until we could make other arrangements.

The fact that Susie and I could work together during this challenging interval highlights a dilemma that "only" children may well face in helping take care of their aging parents. Without siblings to call upon, you may need to recruit the help of other close relatives and/or friends. You also may need to work harder to find all the resources available to your parent in her particular community.

Chapter 4

Coping with Cancer

When a Loved One Has a Terminal Illness

Dad and Mom had been married nearly thirty years when Mom discovered a lump in her breast. She went to the doctor and tests confirmed that she had breast cancer. She was forty-eight years old. They decided to say nothing to my siblings and me.

Soon after Mom's diagnosis, I made my regular Sunday call; I was in grad school at the time. Mom answered the phone, and during our conversation I mentioned coming in for a visit. But Mom was silent. And then I heard Dad say in the background, "I think we should tell Iris what's going on."

Mom reluctantly told me about the lump and her impending surgery. She explained that they didn't want to worry me or burden me by revealing her diagnosis. I was stunned at both her news and their agreement to keep it from their children.

A few weeks later, Dad and I were sitting nervously in the hospital's waiting area while my mom underwent her mastectomy. Time moves so slowly in these kind of situations. You look around at the other people in the waiting area, wondering why they're there. You watch them to see if they seem anxious and are feeling what you are. When it seems like you've been there a long time, you begin to imagine all the things that might have gone wrong. You think about the possible outcomes, speculating on the most frightening one, and wonder how you and your loved ones will cope with it. Then you try to imagine the obstacles and challenges that lie ahead, based on what you'll be hearing from the surgeon. How will your loved one, lying vulnerable on that table, face whatever lies ahead?

Dad had asked me to be there, not just because of my training as a medical social worker, but also for the moral support he clearly needed. He seemed lost; he wasn't sure what to say or what to do. I knew he was scared, but I also knew he wasn't ready to discuss it with me. He was trying his best to be protective of all of us.

Mom's surgeon finally came into the waiting area. In the briefest possible words, he told us that she'd needed a radical mastectomy. In addition, a few of her lymph nodes were found to be cancerous, and he'd removed them. Without waiting for a response from us, he got up and started to walk away.

Stunned by his brevity, I suddenly found myself chasing him—quite literally—along the corridor. Dad and I needed a lot more details: the extent of her surgery, her recovery time, and what this all meant in terms of a prognosis and treatment options. I cornered him—again, literally—so that he couldn't rush off again. This was how we learned that Mom would need to undergo both chemotherapy and radiation.

Communication with my mom's doctors would be an ongoing problem for us as she began her course of treatment. She had total confidence in her doctors and because of this she never asked any questions. She accepted everything they said, without reservation or asking for more information. Her internist would come into the room and tell her how beautiful she looked that day. That was all she wanted and needed to hear.

I'd been working in hospitals as a medical social worker for several years. Respecting the patient's confidentiality is a primary directive to which all health-care practitioners must adhere. Mom seemed to have forged a kind of unspoken agreement with her physicians: she wouldn't ask questions and therefore they would not have to answer them. This was a huge source of concern for my siblings and me. We simply couldn't break through this wall. We wanted to ask specific questions about her prognosis and treatment, but were not allowed to explore any of this. Mom didn't want to offer details. Dad didn't push for answers either.

I would try to prompt my mom to voice any questions she might have. I was sure she did have fears and concerns about her diagnosis and what it meant for her, and that she was afraid to articulate them because she just didn't want to hear the answers. This reticence wasn't consistent with the person we all knew. It left us frustrated and confused. Prior to her diagnosis she had not been shy about expressing her opinions, asking questions, or confronting people when she felt she needed to.

Worse, we'd never really had a discussion with my mother about what to do if she ever became seriously ill. She and my dad had never broached the subject with each other, either. That was surprising as she had moved her mother into our house to take care of her when she'd been diagnosed with cancer. And, she'd had experience with her in-laws who lived with us when they too developed life-threatening medical problems.

The doctors would go to my dad to get his opinion on treatment issues and decisions regarding my mother. He felt uncomfortable making decisions about her treatment, and would ask me to advise him on what to do. In turn, I felt uncomfortable being in this position, but he appeared so overwhelmed. I didn't have the heart to refuse his request.

It's impossible to anticipate how we will respond when faced with a major illness. In my career I saw many families who were very open communicating with each other about the nature of their loved one's illness. Through this experience I've come to feel that the greatest gift a parent can give their spouse and children (when they are the appropriate age) is to have an honest discussion about their wishes regarding the extent and type of medical treatment they want to have.

My dad came to this belief, too. After witnessing what happened with my mom, he felt it was important to have this discussion with us. Candidly, we talked about what he wanted done if he became seriously ill and was not able to make decisions regarding his treatment and care.

Several years ago, I was working in the intensive care unit with a woman who had two adult daughters. She was dying and had not prepared a living will or medical directives. She hadn't discussed anything with her daughters about the type or extent of care she should receive in the event she was seriously ill or incapacitated.

Her daughters had opposing ideas about what type of care she should receive. One daughter wanted to keep her alive with oxygen and feeding tubes. The other daughter believed that her mother wouldn't want to be kept alive in these circumstances. She told the doctor she did not want any extraordinary measures taken on her mother's behalf. The daughters also disagreed about whether their mom should be taken home or remain in the hospital. The doctor didn't know what to do because the daughters had an equal say about her care since their father had died and they were now the closest family.

My work primarily involved talking with the daughters to make sure they understood what the doctor had told them, so that they could make some decisions about treatment options. I wanted to make sure they fully understood their mother's medical condition and her prognosis. We talked about what would happen if she was discharged from the hospital, and the type of help she would need, what it would cost, and who would be available to offer the necessary support and assistance. Eventually the caretaking team was able to help them reach an agreement about the next step. They did bring their mother home, where she received nursing support until her death.

My mom was a stoic woman. She didn't complain much as she faced the harsh results that chemotherapy bestows on many of its recipients. She had terrible sweats and a loss of appetite, which caused her to lose weight. She would frequently throw up. All her hair fell out. Mom's appearance had always been so important to her; she never went out without doing her nails and her hair, and carefully putting on her makeup. So now she bought herself a stylish wig and turban. She continued to do what she could to maintain her regular habits and appearance.

She had lots of help from my dad, other family members, and her group of close longtime friends. They all pitched in to fill the gaps when needed. They helped to get her to and from her chemotherapy treatments. They also made sure she had something to eat when she felt like it. They ran errands and did the grocery shopping to help both my mom and my dad.

After several months, we were given some great news from her doctor. It appeared that her treatment had been successful; her cancer went into remission. Mom regained her appetite, her hair, and her life. We were all incredibly relieved—especially my dad.

Mom jumped back into her routine as if she had never left. We were amazed by her resilience. She joined her friends on their daily shopping excursions. And she also resumed her volunteer work for the Children's Asthma Research Institute and Hospital.

Mom also decided that she wanted something good to come out of her experience battling cancer. She wanted to reach out to other women who might be feeling overwhelmed by the devastating diagnosis of breast cancer. Mom was never at a loss for words, and her subsequent speaking engagements with various local organizations seemed to energize her. She was never shy about sharing her thoughts or her opinions, whether she was asked or not. And so her talks were intimate and honest; she was open to others asking any questions.

Mom touched a lot of lives and was proud of her work and the impact it had on others. She would talk to us about the meetings, the kinds of people who attended, and the questions people asked her. She rightfully believed her story inspired others and offered them and their families new hope. It was my impression that Dad was also glad she had chosen to help others in this way.

The doctors had told us that if my mom remained cancer-free for five years, it would be a good indicator that they had stopped the growth of the cancer, and that she'd have a good prognosis of many more years to come.

But when Mom went for her five-year checkup, her doctor discovered that her cancer had returned. There was also evidence that it had progressed and moved into her bones. We were all devastated by the news.

My mom realized that this meant more rounds of chemotherapy and radiation treatments. She understood that her chances weren't great, but she decided to do any medical interventions that were recommended by her doctors to try to stop the cancer. Dad, my siblings, and I supported her decision.

The chemotherapy took its toll on her. The familiar side effects returned; she suffered from weight loss, chills, severe sweating, nausea, hair loss, and terrible fatigue. She was in a weaker state. This time it was more difficult for her to fight back and recover. If she was angry about the cancer coming back, she never discussed it with us or my dad. As for Dad, he continued to offer her ongoing physical support as she needed it. He also seemed uncertain about what else he could do.

Mom got another wig, and also bought new turbans and scarves. She continued to focus on how she looked. She maintained her daily makeup and nail-polish routines. She'd still be up till 2:00 or 3:00 A.M., trimming her nails, polishing them, gluing on artificial nails. The pungent smell of nail-polish remover was prominent. But we were all happy she returned to her familiar cosmetic regimes. It showed that she wasn't about to give up.

Even as her health continued to deteriorate, she didn't talk about it. Dad didn't say much, either. My siblings and I knew he was frightened. Mom probably did too, but this wasn't a topic we felt we could broach with either of them. It was my impression that the two of them didn't share their fears with each other. Perhaps they were afraid to face the truth, that Mom seemed to be losing this round to the cancer. We knew that Dad didn't want to burden his children—he had told us this very specifically—and this desire was another reason he said so little. Ultimately we all were watching for cues from Mom about how to cope and handle things on a day-to-day basis.

Other, troubling aspects of her illness emerged. Mom began getting more short-tempered. Her memory was impaired at times. Then she began experiencing seizures, which were terrifying to watch. There was nothing we could do to shorten or stop them.

As an observer it feels like it lasts forever. All you can

do is try the best you can to protect the person seizing. Sometimes the person will remember the seizure. Other times they will not. This was true in my mom's case. She had many seizures; her awareness about them varied without any apparent cause.

We eventually learned from the doctors that the seizures were a result of her cancer metastasizing in her brain. This was the worst possible news. Unfortunately, her cancer was not in a part of the brain where an operation could be performed to remove the tumors. She was running out of treatment options—and time.

Mom's moods and her behavior began to be even more severely altered by the cancer in her brain. She became increasingly agitated and mean. She'd swear and scream at us without any warning, with nothing to trigger it. Dad, her main caretaker, silently took the brunt of these abusive outbursts. With increasing frequency she would yell at him and make repeated accusations about things she thought he'd said or done. None of what she said was true or made any sense.

Dad wouldn't argue with her or fight back. I'm not sure he was able to understand that this behavior was due to her illness. But what made it even sadder, and more difficult, is that these outbursts would occur in front of family and friends who were visiting. This was excruciatingly embarrassing for Dad, who was such a private, quiet person. He would simply pretend to ignore her. On the outside he appeared stoic, but we knew that he was experiencing painful emotional turmoil that he kept bottled up inside.

As the months went by, Mom got weaker and continued

to lose weight. She had difficulty standing up and moving around without additional assistance from my dad. He was willing and able to help her with her physical care, despite feeling confused and overwhelmed by her anger and agitation, much of which was directed squarely at him. Mom's physical and emotional decline went on for over a year.

My siblings and I discussed getting outside help for our parents. But Mom refused to allow anyone else in the house to help her. Susie and I offered our assistance, but Dad continued to do most of the caretaking. He too was reluctant to get any outside help. He didn't want to go against my mom's wishes even though she wasn't capable of acknowledging her care needs. She couldn't see the toll it was taking on everyone around her. And Dad was afraid to make her angrier by bringing in professional help.

But as time went on, Mom became totally dependent on him to help with her mobility, her feeding, and going to the bathroom. She became so emaciated that she began to look like a concentration-camp victim.

When you're taking care of a loved one who has a chronic, debilitating illness, you learn what needs to be done. In my own experience with my mom, I felt that completing these tasks contributed to my sense of helpful accomplishment. You just try to get through the day, hoping your loved one's condition won't deteriorate any further. When that happens, it feels like a victory. Inevitably, though, you begin to notice every small thing about how their body is not functioning. There's fear that things will get worse and that there's nothing you can do to stop it. There are moments when you feel helpless. You are grateful when you can ease their pain or help them be more comfortable. The bottom line is that watching a loved one slip away is emotionally and physically draining.

Shortly after Mom's cancer had returned, I began to have sharp, severe stomach pains. Because I was focused on her situation, I ignored them as best I could. But my pain got worse and worse, until finally I went for tests and learned that my gallbladder was in trouble. My doctor told me that I must have it removed immediately, or I'd become incapacitated. So I agreed, and stayed with Susie rather than add an additional burden to Dad's already heavy load.

Susie picked me up after my surgery. I could barely walk, but I asked if we could stop at our parents' house before going on to hers, which was an hour away. When we got to Mom and Dad's, I made my way to their bedroom, where Mom lay in bed. I greeted her, then explained why I wouldn't be able to visit again for a while.

Mom stared at me. "This will be the last time you will be permitted in this house," she answered coldly. "If I wasn't good enough to take care of you, then you are no longer my daughter. When Danny and Caryn come to visit, you'll be allowed here for that. Otherwise you cannot be in this house anymore."

This was the most painful day of my life. I was sobbing. Susie was crying and yelling at Mom; Dad was furious, although even in the midst of all of this emotional turmoil he didn't shout at Mom. The three of us left the bedroom and as we stood by the front door, Dad quietly kept assuring me that of course I would be able to come back to the house.

Suddenly, I really understood, on a deep level, what he'd been going through for all of those months. I could only imagine the toll this had taken on him.

During my recuperation, I was finally able to grasp the distinction between the mother I knew and loved, and the unrecognizable person her brain tumors had turned her into. The mother we knew who loved and cared for us was gone.

Mom continued to grow weaker and her care needs increased. Then one day she had another major seizure. By this point my siblings and I had come to believe that the best thing for her and my dad was for us to make her care decisions for them. Dad wasn't willing to say anything contrary to my mom's wishes. He was fearful of inciting more angry episodes. But it was clear that he was worn out, and that he could no longer effectively manage her care at home. Mom didn't want to go to the hospital, but she did want to have additional treatments if that would slow down her decline. Knowing this, the hospital was now the only place that this could happen safely. It was an incredibly difficult time. Hospital or home? This was one of the hardest decisions my dad or any of us had ever had to face. Finally we decided: hospital.

Mom had been in the hospital a couple of days when, early one morning while Dad and I were visiting her, her doctor told us that she was near death, and that she probably had only a few hours left. I called Susie, and she rushed to the hospital. I also called Caryn and Danny; they both immediately made plans to come to Chicago as quickly as possible.

Mom at this point was in a semiconscious state. I told her I had called my siblings and that they were all on their way. Dad sat quietly in a corner of the room. He wasn't displaying much emotion. He let Susie and me talk with my mom, and with the hospital staff. He just seemed lost.

Our number-one goal was to help Mom stay as comfortable as possible in the brief time she had left. I knew she was experiencing a lot of pain; her cancer had spread everywhere, and she was very weak. I asked her doctor if we could have an order for additional morphine to help manage her pain. I was thankful that he agreed. I knew that it would have a sedating effect on Mom.

Throughout that long day, she seemed to drift in and out of awareness as we all sat by her bed talking with her. We tried our best to comfort her. Gradually her breathing became slower and more labored.

Yet amazing things happened. She hung on for much longer than her doctors had anticipated. And to our joy, the mother we had known and loved returned to us. When she was able to speak to us, it was in a loving way. The harsh anger she'd displayed in the previous year had simply vanished. We held her hand and spoke gently to her, trying all the time to figure out what she needed to keep her as comfortable as we could. We also wanted to allow her to say whatever she wanted to us. We knew this was our final time together. There was nothing that we wanted left unsaid. And Dad spoke with her as well, as we all kept trying to fight back our tears.

Mom was still alive when Caryn and Danny arrived that night. She opened her eyes, and we had no doubt she knew they were there. They both had their own last, brief conversation with our mother, who in turn said good-bye to them.

With the five of us at her bedside, I said softly to Mom, "We're all here now. You can let go anytime you want to."

She died a few minutes later. I will always believe that she chose to wait until we were all together. She felt loved, and so did we.

When a Loved One has a Terminal Illness

In my long experience working in the hospital setting, I have gotten to know many elderly, sick people. I believe that for those who are terminally ill, they often do have a sense of awareness regarding their impending death. Sometimes, it really seems that some people can have control over the moment they die. More than once, I've witnessed the situation where patients whose families were with them constantly seem to wait until the family has left—even if only briefly—to die.

Because of these experiences, it's been important to me to try to understand what happens at the time of death. This understanding, I feel, can help us cope with death and its meaning.

I was fortunate to hear the renowned Elisabeth Kübler-Ross speak about her extensive work with patients who were dying. She is internationally known for establishing the concept of the five stages of grief among those facing death. Kübler-Ross spoke strongly in favor of empathetic touch and its value in caring for dying people. She also believed it's critically important to give such people as much control as possible in order to allow them to die in ways that are meaningful to them. She urged caregivers to talk with people about their impending death, when and if their patients are receptive to it.

When Kübler-Ross began her advocacy work, her philosophies were controversial. But they served to create a whole new awareness of the subject. They certainly were instrumental to me. I came to believe that empathetic touch, and sensitive conversations about death, could be a very important gift for all concerned. People often need a chance to speak about their life, their death, and what they want people to know about them before they die.

Elisabeth Kübler-Ross described situations in which people she worked with waited for family members to be with them when they died. In some of these cases the patients had spoken with her about their fears regarding the hardship on their families watching them die. Some didn't want to die alone. Sometimes the patient needed to hear from a loved one that it was okay to let go and die.

We all must face death at some point. Unless you choose suicide, you are never certain how or when it will happen. It can be sudden and unexpected, or, as with my mom, it can be a long, slow process of deterioration of the body and/or the mind.

The intimacy of being with someone who is ill, and taking care of that person, is both a powerful and painful experience. Your loved one can become increasingly dependent on physical help from others, which can be very difficult for him/her. Also, witnessing that loss of independence is very difficult. Everybody faces their impending death in a unique way.

My mom was fiercely independent. Initially she did not want anyone to offer her physical assistance. As she grew weaker, at some point she reluctantly and tacitly seemed to make the decision to allow us to assist her more with her physical care.

Other people are more verbal about this. They actively want to speak about their fears, feelings, and regrets. They want very much to reflect on their lives. Their terminal condition releases them from the day-to-day societal restraints we all face—the inhibitions that keep us from saying, frankly and openly, what we're thinking or feeling to the people we encounter.

Some people remain quiet or in denial about the severity of their medical condition. It is a similar struggle for family members and friends. Some want to say their good-byes and tell their loved one about the meaning she or he brought into their lives. But uttering these words acknowledges that you know you'll be losing that person. Many dying people simply aren't emotionally or intellectually prepared for this kind of conversation.

I've had the experience of taking care of both family and friends who have lost their battles with chronic, terminal illnesses. When a patient and a caretaker mutually agree to speak openly about the reality of the situation, it can be powerful, emotionally difficult, moving, and rewarding—and sometimes all at once.

The intimate bond that results from knowing that those participating in the process have expressed their wishes, and said everything they needed and wanted to say, brings a closeness and clarity that is truly beautiful. It can be mutually satisfying to those in the midst of it. In my personal life, I have felt privileged to be a part of that process with friends, my father, and other relatives. It doesn't mean there's less pain when they are gone, but the lessons we learn along the way, about how to live our final days, stay with us for our lifetime. And they can offer comfort to those that are left behind.

If your relationship with your elderly, terminally ill loved one has not been a good one, it can be very difficult to achieve this kind of intimacy. As I discussed earlier in this chapter, when my mother was so profoundly argumentative in the final year of her life, it was impossible for me to have that kind of close, comfortable relationship.

If you find yourself in a similarly challenging situation, authors Hugh Delehanty and Elinor Ginzler offer valuable advice in their book *Caring for Your Parents: The Complete AARP Guide*. They recommend the three "A's":

Acknowledgment

The essential ingredient here is good communication. Accept your differences and listen to your parent's opinions. Try not to close the door on sensitive subjects. If your parent wants to discuss his thoughts about death, invite discussion whenever possible and acknowledge his feelings.

Attention

Listening attentively, including making eye contact, is critically important. Being aware of your parent's nonverbal communication—including how she holds her body, whether she is full of tension, and whether she is making eye contact—can tell you much about her state of mind.

Affection

A kiss on the cheek or forehead and a warm smile go a long way in maintaining emotional intimacy. Other physical gestures, like a back rub or brushing your parent's hair, also help.

As my mom went through her battles with cancer, pain management was a critical component of the process. Be sure and consult with your loved one and the doctor or nurse with whom you're working to discuss the most effective options for alleviating pain.

Authors Delehanty and Ginzler offer these suggestions:

- Learn the types of medications your parent might take to alleviate pain. Help him to understand that pain is much easier to prevent than to treat once it becomes severe.

- Be an advocate for your parent. If he isn't assertive enough to tell a doctor or nurse about severe pain, do that for him.

- Help your parent and his caregivers by keeping a record of the time, location, and severity of the pain and the medication that relieved it.

- Understand the dosage that is appropriate for your parent.

- Arrange for your parent to have enough pain medication to tide him over the weekends and holidays.

- Learn about the level of pain medication your parent can expect at the end of life; the amount may increase as the body begins to shut down.

As noted above, it's important to learn from your senior's doctor or nurse about the different options available in pain medications. If you'll be the one administering them, carefully consider what you feel comfortable and qualified to do. For example, some pain medication can be given in drops on the tongue. Others must be given through an intravenous line; this must be done by a nurse.

Hospice care is a very valuable option for people who are coping with end-of-life issues. The hospice philosophy is to offer care for both the patient and family. It views the patient in an integrative way, considering his medical, physical, and emotional needs.

Hospice treatment focuses on giving patients as much dignity as possible as they move through the process of dying. In conjunction with this care, family members are given ongoing educational, emotional, and spiritual support, all of which can help them through this difficult time.

Another key aspect of hospice care focuses on pain management and helping to make the patient as comfortable as possible. Invasive procedures, such as intravenous lines or using devices to restart the heart, are not used. The goal is not to cure the patient. Patients who are eligible for a hospice program have a serious medical condition that is progressive in nature and is not curable.

A typical hospice team includes a physician, a nurse, and a social worker, along with a nurse's aide who assists the patient with personal-care needs such as bathing and bowel/bladder management. Nutrition counseling is also offered in the care plan. The team is available on call around the clock.

Many hospitals and nursing homes offer hospice care. It can also be done at home if the patient wishes to remain there. Regardless of the setting, the hospice team creates a visiting schedule. The frequency of their visits is based on the specific needs of both the patient and their loved ones and/or caretakers.

Medicare usually covers many of the costs for patients who are eligible for hospice care. This includes the cost of equipment such as a hospital bed, wheelchair, or bedside commode. Other insurance may cover some of these costs. You'll need to review your loved one's individual insurance policy coverage. If your loved one doesn't have coverage for needed equipment, try reaching out to your local chapter of the American Cancer Society (and other similar organizations); they may offer what is needed at no cost.

As I mentioned earlier, when a patient enters a hospice program, it's with an understanding that there is agreement not to have any type of extraordinary measures taken to extend his life. For example, if a patient stops breathing, no action will be taken to resuscitate him. The focus is on helping the patient be as comfortable and pain-free as possible.

The Process of Dying

When you spend a lot of time around someone who is in the process of dying, you'll likely become very aware of every aspect of their physical and emotional dynamics. There are common signs that indicate a person is closer to death. Knowing this may help prepare you and your loved one about what to expect as the end of life grows nearer. In *Caring for Your Parents*, authors Delehanty and Ginzler note symptoms to watch for and what to do when they occur:

- The patient may begin to lose interest in eating or drinking. (Use ice chips or frozen juice to keep the mouth moist when swallowing becomes difficult.)

- As the patient grows weaker, she still may want visitors around, but may now prefer a calmer environment with just one or two people around.

- A slowing metabolism makes dying patients less responsive to activity around them or words spoken to them, and they spend more time sleeping. But because they can still be able to hear or otherwise sense their environment, it is important to be with them as much as possible—if only to hold a hand or talk quietly.

- As circulation of oxygen decreases to the brain and other changes associated with dying affect the central nervous system, your parent may experience sensory changes and show signs of confusion or restlessness. Continue to reassure him by talking calmly, touching him, or playing soft music.

- Persons in a coma may still hear what is said even when they no longer seem to respond. Caregivers should act as if the dying patient is aware of what is going on and is able to hear and understand voices.

When death is imminent for your loved one, knowing there are signs and symptoms to look for is crucial to understand what lies ahead. Delehanty and Ginzler describe these symptoms:

- Activity decreases with less movement, less communication, and reduced interest in the surroundings.

- Interest in food and water diminishes.

- Body temperature lowers by as much as a degree or more.

- Blood pressure begins to fall.

- Circulation to the extremities is diminished so hands and feet begin to feel cooler than the rest of the body.

- Breathing changes from a normal rate and rhythm into a pattern known as Cheyne-Stokes respiration: several rapid exchanges of air followed by a period of no respiration.

- Skin color changes to a duller, darker grayish hue.

- Fingernails become bluish rather than the normal pink.

- Speaking decreases. The person ceases to respond to questioning and no longer speaks spontaneously.

- Coma ensues and may last from minutes to hours before death occurs.

In my experience caring for patients who were in a coma, I agree that it's very important to assume they hear and are aware of what you say and do. Once I had a patient who was pronounced dead and was resuscitated. She was able to tell me everything that was done and said by the medical team that brought her back to life.

My work with her and other patients has convinced me that our loved ones often do know what's going on around them, even if they do not appear to. I would quietly talk to patients who were in a coma and gently hold their hands.

What You Can Say and Do

I've helped care for many people who were terminally ill. I've also worked with their families. The truth is, nobody really knows how they will cope with death until they are faced with it. I always urge family members to align themselves with where the patient is in his understanding of his condition, and to not force recognition where it may not be appropriate.

To someone who is dying, having someone who can listen, *really* listen, is so important. I don't recommend that you lie, or make promises you're not able to keep. If you've been advised that your loved one is near death, and she appears to believe that she will conquer her medical condition, it's my suggestion that you simply go with it. If she asks you, "Am I dying?" a good answer might be "I don't know," or "What do you believe?" What you *can* do is help her be comfortable and let her know what she means to you. Try to allow her as much control over her remaining time as possible. Give her the opportunity to say whatever she wants and needs to say.

Another observation I've made in working with the dying is that their lifelong personalities tend to manifest in a more heightened way. For example, people who were mean-spirited and demanding in life become even more difficult as they go through the process of dying. It's very unusual for people to have a huge personality transformation when facing death—a scenario we often see in the movies. It does happen in some cases, for example people facing a great deal of pain or sometimes with patients experiencing Alzheimer's disease. You should be prepared for this possibility.

In addition, toward the end of life, sometimes people can become combative, doing and saying things they never did when they were healthy. This can be very hard on family members observing this.

It may help you to keep in mind that your loved one's independence and privacy is gone as he moves closer to death and needs more hands-on care. Do what you can to preserve his dignity as much as possible. Also, simply saying something like, "Dad, I know your dignity really matters to you, and we're doing our best to maintain it" can really make a difference.

The Time to Talk Is Now

I mentioned earlier how extraordinarily helpful it can be to talk with your aging parent about her future wishes *before* she gets to the point where she's too ill or incapacitated to do so. It can take a huge burden off family members, who must make medical-care decisions, to know in their hearts that they are doing exactly what their loved one would want them to do.

Estate planning is a very important area to explore with your elderly loved one. We'll look at this more closely in Chapter 12, but for now, keep in mind that there are elements of good estate planning that specifically address the issues associated with medical concerns and health care. Living Wills and health-care proxies (also called durable medical power of attorney) are examples of such useful documents. Make sure these documents are properly filled out and completed with the assistance of an attorney that has experience in estate planning. A copy should be kept by your senior, the primary caretaker, and the physician overseeing your senior's care.

Sometimes a person can have an unexpected accident, or the onset of a medical problem can be sudden. In these instances, decisions regarding patient care need to be done quickly by the closest relative or the person designated in these documents. Having a frank discussion *before* this happens is imperative.

Advance Directives for Medical Care

There are many documents that carefully notate end-of-life health decisions. As mentioned above, they include the living will and the health-care proxy; there is also the "do not resuscitate" order.

Living Wills

- Describes the kinds of medical treatments and interventions you do and don't want done.

- Includes specific information about life-sustaining measures you want (or don't want) used, such as ventilators or feeding

tubes. You can add other specific directives
about interventions, too. This document is
sometimes called a "health-care directive" or
"directive to physicians."

Health-Care Proxy

• Names a specific person, sometimes called
  a health-care agent or proxy, who makes
  medical decisions on your behalf if you are
  unable to speak for yourself.

Do Not Resuscitate Order (DNR)

• This document lets your physician and your
  health-care team know that if you stop
  breathing or your heart stops beating, you do
  not want them to perform cardiopulmonary
  resuscitation (CPR) to prolong your life.

• Sometimes referred to as a "no-code order"
  or "do not attempt resuscitation order"
  (DNAR).

To ensure that your DNR is included in your medical
records, consult your physician and attorney.

A DNR order isn't a required element of an advance-directive package, but it does provide important information
to your family and health-care team about your wishes.

The Purpose of Advance Directives

All of these advance-directive documents have a singular purpose—to describe people's wishes in case they can't speak for themselves after an accident or medical problem. They can outline the specific type of care your parent wants ... and doesn't want.

As I mentioned before, it's very important that these types of documents are legally reviewed, properly signed, and in place. You may want to revisit these documents as your loved ones age, in order to ensure that their wishes remain the same. Sometimes as people grow older, they change their minds regarding the kind of end-of-life care they desire.

Having these directives in place provides another additional value. It can give your parents a real sense of control over their final time and how it is managed. This, in turn, may help them more fully accept their end-of-life process.

Importantly, these directives can reduce potential conflict among all those associated with this process. Finally, advance directives can also spare loved ones from having to make heart-wrenching decisions in the midst of a medical emergency. Knowing that a loved one wants treatment withheld in specific, designated situations can alleviate any potential feelings of guilt you might experience.

Requirements for living wills vary between states. Keep in mind, too, that living wills are not put into place until the person who created it becomes incapacitated to the extent that she is unable to indicate what treatment and medical procedures are desired. Make sure your senior parents or other loved ones have a discussion with their doctor about their wishes. Ask them if they would be willing to have you participate in this discussion. It's especially helpful to have their doctor know that you're involved this closely in their care.

Even if a living will is in place, you may want to encourage your elderly loved ones to also consider having a medical power of attorney (POA). Sometimes living wills don't provide sufficient detail; they may lack information that a medical POA can provide, especially regarding end-of-life measures.

When selecting health-care agents, be aware that they can be family members, friends, or legal representatives. Ideally they are geographically close so that they can be consistently involved and present during a crisis in which health-care decisions need to be made rapidly.

You may want to speak with your parents about whether they want the designated health-care agent to be the same or a different person who helps govern their financial affairs when necessary. Family members may have different skill sets or relationships with parents. This may make them stronger candidates for these different but important roles. The takeaway here, and throughout this chapter, is that everyone benefits from planning ahead.

You may want to ask your doctor or hospital if they have any sample forms you can use. In addition, there are also helpful additional resources available in the back of this book.

Chapter 5

Aging and Living Alone

Seniors at Home: Driving, Care Options,
and Medications

After my mom died, Dad found himself living alone in a five-bedroom house. He was sixty-eight years old and in good health. He knew how to take care of himself; the long months of being Mom's primary caretaker had given him experience in doing household chores. At this time in his life, he was content to be in the house he had built and lived in for so many years. It was familiar and safe. He didn't want any more changes. He did what he wanted on his own terms.

The fact that Dad's idea of a gourmet meal was broiled chicken made it all a lot easier. Now that he wasn't limited by having to cook the simple foods my mom had required, his curiosity and courage really took over! He was eager and proud to demonstrate his independence and proficiency in the kitchen. I remember the time he called to excitedly tell me how he'd invented his own beef-stew recipe. My siblings and I would give him well-deserved kudos as he continued to improve on his culinary skills.

In the midst of the severe Chicago winters, Dad was still climbing on the roof to clean the gutters and shoveling the heavy snow that would regularly come. In other seasons, he continued to mow the lawn and pick up the leaves. Maintaining his home was a huge part of how he saw himself. It made him feel good, and it was a frequent topic of conversation when we visited. We were getting concerned about him still doing the heavy lifting and climbing. But he clearly enjoyed it and didn't want to stop. He felt no constraints about his age and didn't see climbing on the roof as any type of risk.

Longtime neighbors had either died or moved away, so there was nobody to check on him regularly except Susie and me.

We were also concerned about how Dad was going to spend his time now that Mom had died. Taking care of her had been his major focus for the last couple of years. It had taken all of his time and energy, and he'd been physically and emotionally taxed by her daily care needs. But now, in the aftermath of Mom's death, I didn't see signs of grief, anger, depression, or sadness. That was worrisome for me. I wasn't sure how he was really doing. In retrospect, I'm sure he had a huge sense of relief. But what I saw at that time was that he didn't go through any type of a mourning period. He didn't talk about my mom at all.

We wanted to respect his feelings, so we didn't discuss anything about Mom in front of him. We understood that he probably still had a lot of residual anger from the way she had treated him during the last couple of years. It made it tough for us to grieve her death, because we couldn't talk about her with him. But we just came to accept that was the way it was going to be.

My dad's most obvious way of coping with her death was to immediately create his own routine. As he had done for decades, he'd get up early, at 4:00 A.M., and make himself some breakfast. Not far from home was a Jewish center that had a health club. He enjoyed going there to work out; not only did it benefit him on a physical level, it was good for him mentally and emotionally, too. It was also a time where he could do some socializing with others. For lunch, he'd sometimes go out to eat. Then, once home again, he'd check on the stock market, watch TV, and catch up on the news before going to bed.

I realized that over the last few years many of my parents' closest friends had died. Having his circle of friends fade away had become Dad's norm. Also, during the time he'd been taking care of Mom, he'd been pretty isolated. He'd gotten used to being alone. He didn't need to be around many other people. As I described in Chapter 1, his brother Jules would frequently come to the house. That was enough companionship for him. They'd sit and watch TV together or go out to eat. Dad's past anger toward Jules seemed to stay in the past. Although they never expressed it within our hearing, it was clear that they needed each other and were grateful for the companionship.

As I mentioned earlier, Susie and I would also come by to check on him, and visit for a while. He also had regular Sunday calls with Danny and Caryn. That was really all he wanted or needed.

Dad was the kind of man who needed to wake up every day knowing he had something to do. He had a close friend named Mickey, who was the head of the local carpenters' union. Mickey became seriously ill and was told he needed a kidney transplant. Dad offered to donate his kidney to help him. When I commented on what a beautiful gesture that was, Dad was surprised. He thought everyone would be willing to do this type of thing for a friend.

As it turned out, Mickey regained his health and didn't need the procedure. And in gratitude to Dad, he invited him to come work at McCormick Place as a member of the carpenters' union. McCormick Place is a huge convention center in Chicago, used for trade shows and conferences. It employs members from a variety of unions such as carpenters, carpet installers, and electricians.

Dad wasn't particularly interested in the money, but he liked the idea of working again at a job—one that wasn't physically demanding.

Dad's job was to help build the booths for trade shows. The vast majority of union members were men. They'd come every day and wait to get picked for jobs. This arrangement was ideal for Dad, because he could work when he wanted to. Carpentry was something he really enjoyed doing, and he could easily do what was expected in spite of being in his seventies.

Dad began referring to McCormick Place as his "stomping grounds." He told me he initially got into trouble because while working on a booth, he noticed there was an electrical cord lying on the carpet that hadn't been plugged in. He was worried that someone would trip over it, so he plugged it in. A supervisor called him over to chastise him, saying, "Only a member of the electricians' union can do that."

Dad said that he quickly learned that doing less was more in this case, and because of his quick grasp of the situation, he was able to fit in, although he did laugh about the rules he thought were silly. We were glad he'd found a place where he could physically do the work, and the fact that it offered some comic relief for him was a bonus.

A year or so after Mom died, Dad started to tell me a story about visiting a bar. I was surprised because it was a bar that I would go to from time to time, so I asked him why he chose that particular place.

"It's time for me to start meeting women to date," he answered calmly.

"Dad," I said, "the age of the people who hang out there are closer to my age than yours. So why are you going there?"

"You're right about the age thing. The other guys in there are a bunch of losers who are scared of women."

"Scared of women? What do you mean?"

"There are all these beautiful women, and nobody was dancing with any of them. I fixed that," he said, laughing.

"How did you do that, Dad?" I asked with some reluctance.

"Well, I scoped out the room to find the prettiest woman there. She was sitting at the bar. So I went up to her and asked her to dance. And she did, of course." With a big smile on his face, Dad added, "That gave those other guys the courage to start asking other girls to dance."

While I was happy that he wanted to start meeting people and dating, I was also a little concerned since he hadn't dated in forty years. He might be an easy target, especially if he chose someone who was much younger than he was. Carefully, I said, "So you want to meet a new lady friend, Dad? Would you like some suggestions about other places where you might meet people that are closer to your age?"

Dad said yes, so I gave him some information about a Jewish singles group that I knew had an older clientele. He followed up and reported back that he was considered a "very hot commodity. Lots of women are interested in me because I'm in good health. I'm a great catch."

Sure enough, a few weeks later he met Ann, a widow who was just a few years younger than he was. She loved dancing and traveling and had shared interests with Dad. They started spending time together. They'd go to places with their singles group where they could have a nice meal and dance, or participate in lots of other group-sponsored activities.

Dad and Ann began dating regularly. He liked to joke and tell us, privately, "If Ann doesn't play her cards right, I'll start playing the field again." We were really happy that Dad had found a lady friend whose companionship he enjoyed. They traveled together and went on several cruises, as well as taking trips to visit Caryn and Danny in California.

I went to visit Dad one day. In a very serious tone, he said, "I want to talk with you about something." I was concerned.

Dad went on to say that ever since I graduated from college and returned to Chicago, he'd tried very hard to respect my independence. "I would never drop in on you unannounced," he said.

I agreed, quickly realizing that Dad was signaling me about the fact that he and Ann were having sex. He didn't want any unexpected visits from his kids. "Would it be all right if from now on, before I come over, I called first?" I asked.

He smiled, gave me a hug, and said that would be just right.

Even though Dad seemed content with his life during this time, one thing became very apparent. He wasn't doing a good job at keeping the house clean. With each visit we saw more obvious evidence of kitchen grease, dust, and dirt. Mold was growing in the bathtub and on the walls of the bathroom. The white carpet turned black in several spots, and newspapers began to pile up.

When we mentioned this, Dad got upset. We tried to get him to hire a cleaning woman, but he didn't want to even consider it. So whenever Susie or I went home, secret cleaning operations occurred. We wondered how Ann could tolerate being there. But it seemed she understood my dad. I'm sure that Ann knew if she said something to him, that would be the end of their relationship.

When Dad and Ann went on vacation, we decided it was the perfect time to bring in reinforcements. I hired a highly recommended cleaning woman. She spent an entire day at the house. Although it looked much better when she was done, it still was far from clean—it was simply more than one person could tackle in a day.

We began to worry about how this deterioration would

affect Dad's ability to sell the house one day, although so far he'd expressed no desire to move.

Dad was still driving and had his car. Usually I did the driving when we were together, but on the occasions during which he drove and I sat in the passenger's seat, I quickly noticed that his driving skills seemed to be getting worse. He'd drive thirty miles an hour in an area with a 50-mph speed limit. His response time was slower. He wasn't as aware of other drivers. I became concerned that he might be one of those people who unintentionally cause an accident.

When I took Dad to the DMV to renew his driver's license, I was confident that he wouldn't be able to—and that it would be a good thing. Dad had a significant hearing impairment. I just figured I could say something to the clerk behind the counter without Dad even hearing me.

I was trying to do just that while Dad had his head stuck in the vision-testing device. I was shocked to learn that his peripheral vision was terrible. He was asked to identify the flashing arrows when he saw them and say where they were, but he couldn't see them at all. This test was supposed to help determine driving competence. To my horror, even though Dad repeatedly failed this test, the clerk kept giving him additional opportunities to take it again.

I quietly mentioned to the clerk that since my father couldn't even see the flashing arrows, perhaps it might not be a great idea to put him back on the road behind the wheel of his car. But it was at that moment that my dad saw *one* arrow flashing and was able to correctly say where it was. The next thing I knew the clerk had stamped his seal of approval, sanctioning Dad's driving application renewal.

Not long after this, however, Dad told me that he didn't feel safe driving anymore, and asked me to help him sell his car. He ultimately gave it to me. We made a deal that I would drive him anywhere he needed to go in the future. We maintained that mutually satisfactory arrangement for a very long time.

When Is It Time to Stop Driving?

There may come a moment when, as your parent's caretaker, you may need to have a candid discussion about safety and not driving. Please consider having this conversation before your parent causes an accident. The consequences of waiting can be deadly.

It is really challenging. For many elderly people, driving their own car represents their ongoing ability to remain independent. Admitting they may not be able to continue driving is an acknowledgment that their physical abilities are diminishing. Some elderly people are unable to recognize or admit their physical or mental decline.

Other seniors may be aware of it, but remain in denial out of fear about the other losses and lifestyle changes associated with this decline.

Some adult children are reluctant to begin this conversation because it may mean they will have to assume more responsibility for their senior's mobility. They're not ready or able to accept what they feel is an additional burden.

Assessing Driving Abilities and Limits: Don't Just Take the Keys

All people age in different ways, and each person should be assessed as to her or his own individual abilities and limitations. Regarding driving ability, the areas that should be evaluated include vision, joint mobility, reaction time, level of alertness, hearing, awareness of surroundings, and memory loss. Hearing is critically important because the driver needs to hear people honking or the sound of a signal at a train stop. Memory loss might cause him problems navigating and could result in him getting lost, possibly frequently.

If your parent has been given a diagnosis of dementia or Alzheimer's disease, she is not capable of doing an accurate self-assessment, and should not be expected to competently participate in this kind of discussion. Anyone given this diagnosis should not be allowed to drive.

The American Association of Retired Persons (AARP) publishes a useful checklist of warning signs to consider if you're trying to figure out when your parents' driving should be limited or stopped. Here it is:

- Almost crashing, with frequent "close calls"

- Finding dents or scrapes on the car, on fences, mailboxes, garage doors, curbs, etc.

- Getting lost, especially in familiar locations

- Having trouble seeing or following traffic signals, road signs, and pavement markings

- Responding more slowly to unexpected situations, or having trouble moving their foot from the gas to the brake pedal; confusing the two pedals

- Misjudging gaps in traffic at intersections and on highway entrance and exit ramps

- Experiencing road rage or causing other drivers to honk or complain

- Easily becoming distracted or having difficulty concentrating while driving

- Having a hard time turning around to check the rear view while backing up or changing lanes

- Receiving multiple traffic tickets or "warnings" from law enforcement officers

Although it may be tempting to just grab the car keys and hide them, it's not the best solution to the problem. You'll be turning this important issue into a power struggle that may result in your parent getting angry and ultimately refusing to even listen to your concerns about her driving safety. You do have other, better options.

One thing you can do is to get in the car with your loved one and observe firsthand how she drives. Use this as a starting point for discussion. This doesn't mean starting a fight in the car! Choose a time when you can sit down together and have a calm exchange.

Tell your parent you love her and that her safety really matters to you. Mention the safety of other people as well. If you've observed her displaying unsafe behavior while driving, use that as an example of a situation during which an innocent person (or people) might have been harmed. Ask her to imagine how she'd feel if other people were hurt, or even killed, because of her driving.

Another possibility to consider is that you may not be the right person to have this conversation with your parent. Is there another trusted relative, or a friend, doctor, or clergy person to whom your senior might be more inclined to listen? Try to enlist that person's help in initiating this discussion. Physicians may be able to do tests in the office that can highlight particular deficits that could contribute to unsafe driving. These tangible signs of incompetency—as opposed to personal opinions—may make the decision to quit driving easier.

You can also try my strategy: going with your loved one for the renewal of his driver's license. I hope you are more successful with the staff than I was. If possible, communicate with the staff about your concerns; ask to speak with a supervisor to discuss your fears and learn about the options for your loved one. She or he may be able to change the license renewal date to a shorter time frame to allow for reevaluation in a more timely way.

Care Options for Seniors Who Are Living at Home

Depending on the type of help your elderly parent needs, there are a variety of levels of care available. If meal preparation is the only issue that seems to be a problem, she might be a candidate for the Meals on Wheels program. Prepared food is delivered right to the person's home at a reasonable cost. (Check with your senior's physician about any dietary issues that should be considered.) You can find out about a local program by calling 888-998-6325 or via the Internet at www.mealsonwheelsamerica.org. In addition, your local senior center or Area Office on Aging should have information about programs near you.

If your senior is able to remain at home but you feel it would be rewarding for him to have some socialization time, prepared meals, and the opportunity to engage in stimulating activities, adult day-care programs may be a good option. These programs often provide transportation. In *Caring for Your Parents,* authors Hugh Delehanty and Elinor Ginzler offer these recommendations about what to look for in an adult day-care program:

- Assesses your parent's abilities and needs before admission.

- Has a range of services such as transportation, health screening, personal care, meals, and counseling.

- Provides an active, individualized program that meets your parent's social, recreational, and rehabilitative needs.

- Provides referrals to other community services for older adults.

- Has well-trained, well-qualified staff and volunteers.

- Meets or exceeds existing state guidelines.
- Has clear criteria for terminating services.

- Has a clean facility.

In order for your loved one to be eligible for this type of program, she cannot be combative or demonstrate serious behavior problems. She also cannot be at risk for roaming or leaving the premises, since the staff may not be able to provide that additional level of supervision. So if your parent has been diagnosed with dementia or Alzheimer's disease, be sure to ask if the center has guidelines regarding such participants. Also, make sure you understand what, if any, fees are involved.

Meeting the Challenges Created by Long Distance

In her book *How to Care for Aging Parents*, Virginia Morris points out that "at least a third of all family caregivers care from afar—at least an hour away and usually four or more hours. About half of caregivers work either full-time or part-time."

As I've mentioned elsewhere, the challenges of long-distance caretaking are greater. You'll need to deploy a lot of organizational skills to create a successful care plan for your aging parent or parents. An important step is to identify friends or other family members, who live nearby who can be partners on your caretaker team. These people should have a key or know the security code to get into your senior's home in case of an emergency. Also, they should be willing to visit on a regular basis to observe firsthand how things are going.

If you are unable to find anyone to do this, you may want to consider hiring a geriatric care manager. These individuals have expertise in working with the elderly. They're able to assess what is needed and link a senior with the appropriate resources and support. In addition, they're available to follow up and monitor the home situation to ensure that the plan that's been put in place is working. And finally, if something unexpected occurs, like an aide not showing up, a geriatric care manager can help you figure out how to adjust your senior's care plan accordingly.

To find someone in your area, contact the Aging Life

Care Association, formerly the National Association of Professional Geriatric Care Managers. They can provide referrals. The phone number is 520-881-8008 and their website is www.aginglifecare.org.

Creating a Lifeline in Emergencies

Emergency-response devices can provide an additional measure of comfort and safety. Security companies, such as ADT, MedicalAlert, and Lifeline, offer these systems. Infrared motion sensors are placed in numerous places around your loved one's home. Designed to detect changes in temperature or movement, they continuously transmit information about the movements of the people in the home. If there is a sudden disruption, a company responder will call to make sure everything is all right. If nobody responds, the responder will contact the police or emergency medical services to check on the status of the designated individual. However, if the responder can speak directly to the person and is able to identify the nature of the problem, he or she will dispatch the appropriate support. In addition, a designated family member can arrange to be contacted in an emergency situation.

There are also devices that can be worn like a necklace; they feature a button that can be pressed in the event of an emergency, such as a fall that prevents the wearer from getting up again. The device sends out a signal to a designated recipient, such as a family member or an emergency dispatch center. A phone call is then made to find out if help is needed. These devices are invaluable for people who fall and can't manage to reach a telephone or an emergency pull cord.

Some emergency response systems come with special telephones that have a speaker component, allowing security-company staff to talk with the senior to get information on his condition. If the senior doesn't respond, emergency medical personnel will be dispatched to the home. There is a wide range of options associated with these systems, so prices vary quite a bit—from $150 to $2,000 per year. You should expect to pay an installation fee no matter what system you choose.

Keep in mind that you also have the option of renting an emergency response system on behalf of your senior. Many people like this option because it gives you a chance to test the system with your senior to see how he adapts to it. Another advantage is that if there's any type of equipment failure, you are not responsible for fixing it. The company should do that. If you do have problems, you're able to terminate your agreement.

Your local senior center or state department on aging should have information that will help set up this service; you can also contact your local hospital to see if their social work department can assist you. They may have info on how you can get discounted rates.

In *How to Care for Aging Parents*, Virginia Morris offers helpful information regarding specific questions you should ask as you investigate the best emergency response system for your loved ones:

When comparing companies, ask questions about the staff that's receiving emergency calls. Are they available twenty-four hours a day? How are they trained? Do they speak your parent's native language? Find out the company's average response time. How often does the center test the system to be sure it is working? Where do the calls go when a signal is sent? Ask if your parent can try the system for a trial period or get a money back guarantee. Find out about warranty, cancellation, service and repair policies. What happens if your parent moves? What happens if your parent cancels a lease agreement? What happens if the system is faulty?

Care Options for Help at Home

Sometimes seniors need some additional help with basic things like grocery shopping, laundry, cooking, and/or making sure they can safely take a bath and get dressed.

But what about more complicated care needs such as supervising skin care or checking intravenous lines? These too can also be managed at home, but they must be done by a registered nurse. Especially if you're a long-distance caregiver, and you can't always rely on local family and friends, you may need to bring in professional help. Hiring the right person is very important.

Here is an overview of the different levels of care. These types of health providers are available in most areas of the country.

Registered nurse (RN)

He/she offers the most skilled level of care and is trained to administer medication, handle intravenous lines, manage skin care, and take vital signs, such as temperature and pulse rates. She also provides wound care and catheter care. RN services are the most costly. Depending on the patient's diagnosis, Medicare may cover the cost.

Licensed practical nurse (LPN)

Different states have different rules about the type of care an LPN is allowed to provide, although *all* LPNs can give medication, take and record vital signs, and offer wound care and dressing changes. In many states they can start intravenous lines and maintain them. If they are providing skilled care, Medicare may cover this on a short-term basis.

Nurse's aide, also called "nursing assistant"

Her role includes helping with skin care and incontinence issues. She also assists with bathing and dressing, as well as monitoring a patient's safety and balance problems, if any.

Companion

This type of caregiver may not have medical training. His role is to offer companionship and to monitor safety. He can also help with a variety of domestic tasks including meal preparation and other chores around the house. Medicare does not cover these services; Medicaid may help cover some of them.

The cost of these services will vary depending on the frequency of visits or if the caregiver is there full-time as a live-in.

Homemaker

This type of caregiver is neither licensed nor certified. She can assist with home chores such as laundry, meal preparation, and helping the senior with dressing. She can also help monitor safety and falling concerns.

All states offer some form of in-home care support for seniors on a longer-term basis. These programs, called Home and Community-Based Services (HCBS), are available for Medicaid recipients who have mental, physical, intellectual, or developmental limitations. If they are able to meet these category guidelines, they may be eligible for Medicaid funding.

For your senior to be a candidate for this type of assistance, he must be able to demonstrate that there's a specific need for care. This can be done with the help of his physician. HCBS will review your senior's requirements for medical care as well as for help with non-skilled care such as bathing, dressing, and/or meal preparation.

To be eligible, people requesting these services must have limited assets and be in a lower-income bracket. Guidelines vary among the states. Home-care agencies can offer more specific information regarding your state's regulations and requirements.

For more details about HCBS, contact your local Medicaid office. Contact information is available for each state online at: www.benefits.gov/benefits/browse-by-state. In some cases, an HCBS-affiliated program may be able to pay a family member to provide a senior living at home with non-skilled assistance.

When considering hiring an agency or a private-duty caretaker to come into your loved one's home, be sure and ask a lot of questions, especially concerning prior experience. Do a background check to make sure the person you're considering doesn't have a police record or a history of doing things you would not be comfortable with. It's always advisable to do this type of research before you let a stranger into your parents' home. Here are some useful questions to ask a prospective caregiver:

- Have you taken care of someone with a similar diagnosis and similar care needs?

- How long have you been doing this?

- For how long have you been affiliated with this agency?

- Is the agency bonded? (This is important, as it signifies that your seniors are protected should an employee of the agency steal from them.)

- Do you charge on an hourly or a daily basis? Is there a written contract for our agreement?

- Are you certified with Medicare and Medicaid? If so, do you bill them or do I?

If you're considering hiring a caregiver who is not affiliated with an agency, keep in mind that Social Security taxes will be an issue. Cheryl Kuba covers this in her book *Navigating the Journey of Aging Parents: What Care Receivers Want.*

She also discusses other things you'll want to talk to a caregiver about, such as setting up a payment schedule, if meals are included as part of his wage, your policy about smoking, access to a private bedroom and bathroom, and if he will be responsible for pet care. Kuba also mentions vacation/holiday pay, if the caregiver can have visitors while watching your loved one, and coverage for when the caregiver is off duty.

Coping with Costly Medications

The cost of medications is a huge issue for many seniors, especially for those who are taking multiple medications. If this is an issue for your loved one, your physician may be able to help. He might be able to offer free samples. Also, some pharmaceutical companies offer reduced costs for certain customers who meet income criteria. Contact them to inquire about your senior's eligibility.

As a military veteran, my dad received a pharmacy discount card from the Veterans of Foreign Wars. This card allows recipients to save up to 75 percent on many FDA-approved medications at over fifty thousand pharmacies around the country. For example, at a certain point in his life, Dad's cost for his two medications was $137 a month. When I brought his VFW card to his pharmacy, his cost dropped to $40. You can learn more about this by calling 888-854-1317 or via the Internet at www.thehealthcarealliance.com/vfw.

Is your loved one a member of a large organization such as AARP? Medication discounts are often included in the cost of membership. Inquire at your parents' pharmacy or check with their group(s) about their potential eligibility.

Many medications have a generic counterpart; these are often less expensive. Talk to your pharmacist or doctor about whether the generic version is as effective as the brand-name medication. As you always should do, ask about side effects and potential drug interactions.

You may be surprised to learn that the price of medications in pharmacies can vary quite a bit. If costs are a concern for your loved one, it may be worth it to shop around and compare prices. At GoodRx.com, you can type in your prescription and the site will display comparative prices from your local pharmacies, as well as offer coupons and savings tips. It may also help to call your local pharmacies to get current accurate information as drug costs can change.

Talk to your senior's pharmacist or doctor about other strategies for offering quality care at reduced costs. For example, if your senior orders a prescription in three-month quantities, it may cost less than a month-to-month refill. Sometimes there's more than one medication available to treat a specific medical problem. One medication may be covered under your senior's pharmacy plan while another may not. If she needs a 50 mg daily dose of a medication, it may be cheaper for her to get it in 100 mg doses and then cut the pill in half. Your pharmacist might be willing to help you with this, so that it doesn't have to be done at home, where mistakes can happen.

What Do You Need to Know about Medicare?

Medicare is usually available to people over the age of sixty-five regardless of their financial assets. People with disabilities under that age can also be eligible. Those who receive Social Security benefits are automatically enrolled for Medicare Parts A and B.

Part A of Medicare covers inpatient hospital care, skilled nursing facility care, home health care, and hospice care. It is important to note that this does not mean unlimited care for all of these areas. For example, in order to get coverage in a skilled nursing facility, you must have been hospitalized for at least three days. Your care in the nursing home must be for the same condition or a related medical problem. Finally, you must need skilled care, which is doctor ordered care, offered by a licensed professional. Examples of this are physical, occupational, or speech therapy. The therapists must be able to document your progress in order to continue getting coverage.

Hospice care can be covered under Part A of Medicare if a hospice doctor and your medical doctor certify that you have a life expectancy of six months or less. You must agree to palliative or comfort care instead of active or aggressive treatment to cure your medical condition. You must also sign a statement confirming you are selecting hospice care instead of other Medicare covered treatment for your medical problem.

Part B of Medicare covers outpatient services considered medically necessary by your physician. These services can be delivered in a hospital, doctor's office, clinic, or other health facility. In addition to services like doctor visits, laboratory tests, or X-rays, Medicare Part B also covers medical equipment, like wheelchairs or walkers.

You should discuss what coverage you are eligible for with your health-care provider or the person working with your provider who processes insurance claims and does billing. Ask about your specific diagnosis and recommended treatment to determine if you have coverage and how long the coverage will be available.

There is a premium associated with Medicare Part B; people have the option of choosing not to take it. It's under Medicare Parts A and B that your senior can get coverage for home health-care services, such as a visiting nurse and/or physical, occupational, or speech therapist visits. These services are covered on a short-term basis as long as the health-care providers can document patient progress and care needs. For more information, go to: www.medicare.gov/files/ask-medicare-questions-and-answers.pdf. There are Medicare savings programs. For a premium and drug copay, Medicare Part D offers coverage to help pay for prescription medications. Your elderly loved one may be eligible for prescription discounts from Medicare's Extra-Help or her state Medicaid program if she meets income requirements and other guidelines.

State programs can provide help with Medicare premiums. One helpful program that's offered through Medicare and Medicaid is the Program of All-Inclusive Care for the Elderly (PACE); it provides financial assistance for a variety of medical support services (including prescription drug coverage) in order to help people remain at home, rather than having to go to a nursing home.

Medicare savings programs can also provide financial assistance to help with the costs of premiums, prescriptions, and copayments. Examples of these are the Qualified Medicare Beneficiary (QMB) Program and the Specified Low-Income Medicare Beneficiary (SLMB) Program. To learn more about these programs and other ways to cut costs, go to www.medicare.gov and review these pages:

- www.medicare.gov/your-medicare-costs/ help-paying-costs/save-on-drug-costs/save-on-drug-costs.html

- www.medicare.gov/your-medicare-costs/ help-paying-costs/get-help-paying-costs.html

Chapter 6

Transitions: Leaving Home

Finding the Right Assisted-Living Community

My dad was sixty-nine when my mom died. For eleven years after that, he continued to live independently, but as I described in Chapter 5, it got harder and harder for him to keep up with the maintenance on his home. For one thing, it just got dirtier. We also saw that as the carpet began to tear in places, Dad would simply tape it down.

My siblings and I knew that Dad couldn't go on like this indefinitely. But it was very tough to know when and how to begin the conversation about selling the house. We were certain that the time had come, but we also wanted Dad to feel that he could make his own decisions at his own pace. But our hesitation ultimately proved to be a mistake.

In the fall of 2002, I came home from a vacation and called Dad to check in and let him know I was back. "So," I asked casually, "what's new?"

"I sold the house," he answered, just as casually.

I was stunned. "What did you just say?"

"I sold the house."

Almost at random, I said, "Did you get the price you hoped for?"

"Yes, I did, and more."

"When do you have to be out of the house?"

"Three weeks."

I asked the next logical question. "Where do you intend to go?"

Dad laughed. "There are lots of places out there," he said calmly. "I was hoping you would help me find one."

Frankly, I was still trying to take in the "three weeks" part. I kept thinking about a house that had been lived in for over fifty years. It also held the inherited possessions from five dead relatives, whose things were stored in the basement. The good news, I reflected, was that my siblings and I didn't have to initiate that conversation we'd been dreading. The bad news was that I had to act at lightning speed to figure out how to make it all happen.

I was panicking, but Dad was calm and optimistic. "I have faith in you, Mighty," he said. That was the nickname he had given me. I needed to be that and more. Thank goodness Susie was willing and able to help.

I did some research and found a reputable professional in the estate-sale business. And as I began polishing the enormous collection of silver items my mom had accumulated, I felt like a Disney character before she became a princess. It took me over a week just to get the polishing done.

The process that followed was arduous, chaotic, and deeply emotional for Susie and me. We reviewed in detail with Dad what he wanted to sell and what he wanted to keep. He was planning on moving to a small apartment, which meant that pretty much *all* of the contents in the house needed to be taken by us kids, sold, given away, or thrown out. The day of the sale was the hardest, but in the end Dad received almost exactly what the estate-sale person had estimated, and he was pleased.

I knew we wouldn't be able to sell all of Dad's possessions at the estate sale. I found a company that would be willing to take everything that was left for a flat rate of $300. They came to look at what was there, and we made a plan for them to come back, five days before Dad had to vacate the house. On the appointed day, I waited for them, but they didn't show up. I called, and we arranged for them to come the next day. They were late. And when they finally arrived, they were in a *car*. Not in a truck, but a car.

I was so angry that I went down to the basement where there was a leather couch they'd expressed interest in having. I walked into Dad's old workshop, picked up a hacksaw, and started sawing the couch in half. It was a surprisingly soothing activity. Just as I had pretty much cut the couch in half, the Three Stooges (as I dubbed them in my mind) came downstairs and found me.

"Did you do that?" one of them said, awed.

I smiled what must have been a very menacing smile.

They leaped into action. Two hours later the entire house was cleared out, including the two separate pieces of the couch.

The house was now empty, and Dad was more than ready to take the next step.

While all this had been going on, we also had to quickly determine the right place for Dad to live. At first, he wanted to move into an apartment. But it became clear that, given his desire to not spend a lot of time cooking, this might not be the best choice. Also, Dad wanted a place where he could continue to exercise, as he'd been doing for many years at his community center. And third, he needed to be in a situation where his girlfriend, Ann, could comfortably visit him.

On the plus side, Dad had no immediate health problems. He wasn't even on any medication. However, we all knew he wasn't going to get any younger.

It really helped that he was willing to have a frank discussion about what he was able to do and what he didn't want to do. I did my research and found three assisted-living facilities that were close to me. That was an important consideration since I would be the one who most frequently visited Dad. These programs had a dining room, so Dad wouldn't have to cook. They also had workout facilities. It was a perfect solution, especially since he'd have access to nursing services if he needed them.

The downside? I knew Medicare wouldn't pay for any of it. Dad would have to dip into his personal savings to cover the costs of living there.

We went to the first place. With a staff person as our tour guide, we proceeded to a model apartment. Dad got the ball rolling immediately. "I have a lady friend," he told her, "and she does spend the night sometimes, and we make noise. I want to make sure that won't be a problem here." I wanted to melt right into the carpet and disappear, but with total aplomb the staff person assured my dad that no, it wouldn't be a problem.

In the days that followed, I narrowed our search to two places. The next step was to arrange for Dad to eat at each one, as food was so important to him.

During these visits, I discreetly spoke with the residents and their family members to get their feedback. Ultimately Dad picked the facility which offered, in his opinion, the best food and the best gym. He selected a one-bedroom apartment. He declared his intention of getting up at his regular time—four in the morning—to go do his workout. I was concerned about him likely being the only person in the gym, but the staff assured me there was a camera in there with security staff watching twenty-four hours a day. It made me feel safer knowing that if something happened, he would get immediate assistance.

Once Dad made his selection, the facility sent a staff person to his house, where she looked at the furniture he was planning to bring, then put together a blueprint so that it could all be comfortably arranged in his new apartment.

Dad's move went smoothly and seamlessly. He didn't care that his apartment was small. Very quickly he created a new routine for himself, which he followed with military precision. He did his workouts regularly and ate his meals at the same time every day. He loved having someone else prepare his food. He also enjoyed getting to choose what and when he would eat. This became a daily highlight for him. And he was very proud of the fact that the security guard would salute him whenever he saw him. The guard had told Dad how impressed he was with his faithful exercise regime.

Describing himself as a "lone wolf," Dad wasn't very interested in meeting other residents. He commented to me one day that all of his friends had died; I couldn't blame him for not wanting to go through the pain of making new friends only to lose them as well. However, he did cheerfully acknowledge he would be very sought after by the women there. "I'm a very desirable catch," he'd say with a smile.

Part of Dad's new routine included weekly visits from Ann. (He told me not to visit him on those days, and, mindful of his earlier disclosure to the staff person, I readily agreed.) Dad liked that when Ann was there, he could treat her to a "free meal" since he sometimes skipped meals and got credit added onto his account.

Dad lived in this facility for about five years. Lots of staff changes, along with a decline in the quality of the food, displeased him. One day he called me and said decisively, "I'm out of here. I'm tired of this."

"Where do you want to go, Dad?"

"I'll just take an apartment somewhere nearby."

Clearly, he hadn't thought it out. I refrained from blurting out, "That's a ridiculous plan." My siblings and I were incredibly lucky that Dad respected us and did value our opinions. It helped balance out our reversal of roles when we suddenly had to "parent" him.

I didn't like to tell him what to do. But I did ask him several key questions that struck an immediate chord. "Do you plan on cooking every day? Are you going to go grocery shopping in the winter without a car? Where are you going to work out?" That stopped him in his tracks. There was a pause and then he told me, "I heard about a place further up along the lakefront."

Well, at least that gave me a starting point. Somewhere near Lake Michigan on Lake Shore Drive there was a place my dad was interested in.

I got right on it. But I also bluntly advised him that I did not plan on helping him move again; he'd better be sure about this next place he picked because unless something unexpected happened, he was going to die there. These moves, even in his downsized condition, were still a big job. They took a toll on Susie and me. What Dad didn't realize, either, was that he'd have to adjust to a new environment, new staff, and a different routine. This would not be an easy transition for him at his age.

One of the things I discovered as I began my research was that it was a very competitive market. These types of housing programs are eager to take on new residents. They don't make money on apartments or rooms that are vacant. Sometimes residents die, or move, or leave for a variety of other reasons. This gave me some additional leverage. Once I found the place that Dad alluded to, we went together to check it out. They gave us a tour that ended in the dining room, where Dad dove into the menu. As I had when we'd first toured these facilities, I took some time to talk with some of the residents in the dining room. When all was said and done, Dad decided he loved the food and the apartment. He also liked the fact they had a men's club and special programming for veterans. We met with the administrators and arranged for him to move in.

Dad really liked his new home. It surprised us how quickly and easily he adapted. It helped that he had an action plan for making it happen. The first thing he did was spend time getting to know the staff that ran the dining room. He even met the cooks, whom he complimented on their fine cuisine. He also introduced himself to the woman in charge of seating in the dining room. In his eyes, her job was very important; if he had a problem he could go directly to her. As he explained to me, "You have to make friends with the right people." He made it a point to be the first person in the dining room so he could have good service. This also allowed him to sit where he wanted to.

I followed Dad's lead and got to know the administrator, the head nurse, the staff in the therapy department, and the concierge at the front desk. They all became like an extended family for Dad and for us, too. The staff knew my dad very well, and he, in turn, felt comfortable with them.

When problems occurred, we had these solid relationships in place. They were more than willing to go the extra mile for my dad. I could call Gwen, the concierge, at any time and ask her if she had seen my dad and how he was doing.

My dad did make one new friend in his new home. He referred to him as "the Irishman." I later learned his name was Rob. Together they ventured out into the neighborhood and discovered an Irish bar that served Guinness beer. My dad thought this was a special treat. After his first foray, he told me, "We made friends with the bartender there and he took real good care of us."

Dad and Rob developed a daily ritual. They would sit together outside the dining room so they could be the first ones for meals. But they would sit at separate tables, right next to each other, while they ate and sometimes conversed.

I thought that was pretty odd. "Aren't you and Rob friends?" I asked.

"Yes, we are."

"Well then, why don't you eat together?"

"It's simple. We're both lone wolves," he explained. "Also, that way people understand we don't want to have company at meals. I wouldn't want people to get the wrong idea and have some woman come and sit down with me. I'd never be able to get rid of her after that."

Both my dad and Rob mutually agreed as to the wisdom of this arrangement, so who was I to argue?

Finding the Right Assisted-Living Community

There are several issues to consider if your senior is thinking about transitioning to a new home; a key one is determining the right level of help that he'll need. You may want to gather information from his physician and/or people who spend time with him—especially if you haven't personally been able to see how he functions in his home environment. Remember that a senior's own reports about how he manages on a daily basis may or may not be accurate.

Here's a checklist that will help as you're considering this next, significant step for your senior:

- What is her medical history?

- Does she have any physical limitations?

- Does she have problems with physical mobility? For example, going up and down steps, getting in and out of bed, standing from a sitting position, getting in and out of a bathtub?

- How well can she complete daily self-care tasks such as dressing, bathing, and meal preparation?

- Does she have problems with short- or long-term memory?

- Does she have problems with bowel or bladder incontinence?

- Does she have cognitive problems such as forgetfulness, uncertainty about the time/date, or knowing where she is?

- Is she having difficulty keeping accurate and

up-to-date information about finances? Is
she paying bills on time and staying on top
of her checkbook and bank records?

- Do you feel there are behavioral concerns,
  such as agitation, paranoia, depression, anxiety,
  and/or decreased ability to function at night?

- Do you have any concerns about alcohol or
  drug abuse?

- Is she on any medications? Does she understand their purpose? Can she take them
  properly, without any type of supervision?
  Can she get her prescription refilled?

- Regarding her current home situation, is it
  being properly maintained? Does she have
  appropriate food?
- Is she able to manage the cleaning of
  her home?

- Does she have a car? Is she able to safely
  drive? Are there other types of transportation
  that she can easily and safely use?

- Considering these questions and your
  answers, do you think your senior needs
  supervision in order to remain safe and well
  cared for in her current home environment?

If possible, your senior should be a part of this conversation, along with your siblings (if any), other family members, and close friends.

Sometimes all that's really needed is to simply downsize from a home that has become too onerous for your loved one to handle. Living in a smaller home, apartment, or condominium can offer relief from maintenance challenges.

When helping your loved one find a different living space, top on your list should be a place with no stairs and easy accessibility. Look for doors that are a wider width, should a walker or wheelchair become necessary. Bathrooms should have tubs and/or showers that are easy to get in and out of; handrails are a must.

Another consideration should be location. How great a distance is it to family and friends? Are there nearby grocery stores and pharmacies that can also deliver? Are your elder's preferred doctors nearby?

Additional Insights about Assisted Living

If staying at home is no longer an option for your loved one, an assisted-living facility might be a good choice. Residents can live in their own rooms (sometimes with a roommate) or apartments, and go to a common dining room for meals. Sometimes the units are also equipped with kitchens.

In order for your loved one to be eligible for assisted living, she cannot have any history of "management" or behavior problems. She also cannot be at risk for roaming or leaving the premises since required staffing may not offer the proper level of supervision. Find out if there are any guidelines regarding participants who may have dementia or Alzheimer's disease. Remember to ask about all fees associated with the program including transportation.

At this sort of facility, various recreational and social activities are typically offered every day. Transportation may be available. Help twenty-four hours a day is generally offered. A nurse is on staff, and there may also be a rehab area that provides the services of a physical and/or occupational therapist. Often there are support staff and aides to assist with laundry, bathing, and personal care. If residents wish to have companions live with them, this is usually permitted.

Residents pay rent for their units; support services come with additional fees. If a doctor refers a resident for physical and occupational therapy based on certain medical diagnoses, Medicare does cover 80 percent of the costs for these services.

Some assisted-living facilities offer varying levels of care. For example, if a resident becomes ill and incapacitated, she can be transferred from her apartment to a different area that offers nursing-home type care with higher levels of supervision.

These programs may require residents to purchase a unit. In exchange, the resident is guaranteed that whatever level of medical help he'll need will be provided. The premise is that this is the one place a resident will live regardless of the medical problems he'll face. This can be a particularly good arrangement for couples; if one person needs more assistance and must transfer to a different area, they can still live in close proximity to each other. It relieves the caretaker burden that may arise for the healthier partner. The person who experiences a medical problem can move back to his apartment when appropriate per doctor's orders and the facility's guidelines.

An assisted-living community can provide a safe environment for residents. It also gives a measure of comfort for residents and family members knowing that some type of help is available night or day.

Keep in mind that moving from their home to a new place is a significant, even traumatic event for some elderly people. Be sure to give your parents the opportunity to talk about their feelings, and if possible, allow them to be active participants in this transition, so they'll feel they're very much a part of the process. Make sure they have the contact information for various staff members if concerns or problems arise.

Expert Advice on Assisted Living

Edie is a nurse and the geriatric specialist in charge of the wellness program at an assisted-living facility I was familiar with. I knew she'd be able to provide some great insights for *Role Reversal*, and she very kindly agreed to be interviewed.

I started off by asking her to describe her facility's typical residents.

"Most are starting to lose their independence and are increasingly frail," she answered. "Basically they're independent in some things, but may need help with two or more activities of daily living. They may need help with medication or getting to appointments. Or they may have memory issues."

"What recommendations should we give family members who are assisting their parents in finding appropriate placements?" I asked.

"The Internet can be a great tool, but you have to be careful. Geriatric care managers can really help with the search, although they can be expensive." Edie went on, "If your parent is leaving the hospital, there is help from social workers who do discharge planning. If he or she is already in a retirement community, then of course a nurse there can help with assessment. If you're the one doing a lot of the research, it helps to talk with someone who's been through it. Call people; network. Even if a certain place comes highly recommended, make sure you go out and take a look at it."

We spoke about the importance of finding the right facility for a loved one.

"Yes, you need to know what your parent's priorities are regarding a facility," Edie agreed. "You need to know what the facility offers. What are your parent's care needs? What are his finances? This will help you find the best match. It's not an easy task. You need to allow yourself time to do the legwork so that you're not forced into making a hasty decision because of time pressures or other circumstances such as discharge demands from a hospital. Initiate the process as early as possible. If you can, bring your parent with you."

We discussed the greatest challenges facing families and their aging parents as this placement process is initiated.

"The biggest challenge is often a financial one," explained

Edie. "Assisted living can cost six thousand dollars a month." There can be emotional challenges too. "Sometimes new residents come in with a lot of anger about leaving their homes and coming to a place like this. It used to be when people left their homes and went to a retirement community, that was great because they could enjoy their retirement. It still *can* be true, but people are living longer now. When they come into an assisted-living community, people are telling them what time they have to go to eat, or when they have to go to the bathroom if they're on an incontinence-training program." She went on, "When an independent person comes into a place with rules, it can be difficult for them to give up that control."

Edie and I talked more about the atmosphere in an assisted-living community and the wide variety of residents typically living there, with an assortment of skill levels, abilities, and limitations. "We have people who are independent and people with twenty-four-hour caregivers. It's complicated, because the independent people don't really want to see all those walkers and wheelchairs in the dining room." She added, "It's a dynamic environment. People do often go from being independent to being someone who needs the highest level of care."

That really rang true for me. I remember when my dad, at that time in his eighties, complained, "There are just too many old people here." He didn't feel he should be living among seniors with—as Edie mentioned—wheelchairs and walkers. It took time for him to adjust. Ultimately he became a person needing a cane and, later, a wheelchair. I was glad he lived in a place that allowed whatever devices were needed to help maintain the residents' safety and independence. And in fact, his own change in circumstance gave him a different and more positive perspective on his environment.

I asked Edie, "What do residents need most from family members to help them be as independent as possible?"

"All family members need to understand that when their family member is brought to a facility like this, they still need to advocate for them. Often they can't advocate for themselves. So the family still needs to be involved. It's important to take their loved one out to lunch or dinner. Bring the grandkids here. Coming here is a huge change, and it's very important that a resident stays familiar with family. If you feel burnt out from caregiving, then let us do it. We want to take that burden off the adult children."

"What questions should people ask when they're trying to find an assisted-living facility or nursing home?" I asked.

"You want to know everything and see all the services that are available," said Edie. "You want to come look at the facility and know what size room or apartment they're getting. You need to know what things cost. This is very important especially if they're on a fixed income. Find out what's available for your parent through sources like Medicare and Medicaid. Medicaid won't pay for assisted living, but will pay for subsidized living. You want to be honest about your parent's financial situation. And just like when you go to a specialist, write your questions down. Also, be honest about the type of activities your loved one needs assistance with. This helps you have an accurate picture of what special care is offered and what the costs will be for your senior."

Finally, we discussed the most common mistakes she sees new residents make as they move in and try to adjust to the community.

"Some people move in and they don't want to come out of their apartment," commented Edie. "So we have to get them out and meeting people. We have resident activities so they can meet new people. I worry about depression, which is a common problem. They're afraid of losing their independence, so we try to help them change their mindset a little. The thinking shifts: 'Even though I can't do everything on my own, I know that somebody can come and assist me to go to dinner.' They'll see they can have a really good meal there, and maybe they'll want to learn more about cooking from our cooking classes."

You May Have Surprising Bargaining Power

Earlier in this chapter I described how my dad was very reluctant to meet new people when he first moved into assisted living. But I felt strongly that making new connections would be beneficial for him. And I knew that his being a soldier in World War II was very important to him. I've already mentioned the closeness he felt with his fellow soldiers. So when we were looking at an assisted-living facility, I asked about other male residents who had served in World War II. The staff arranged for him to meet two wonderful gentlemen who were WWII vets. He met them during our initial visit. They exchanged war stories and later participated with my dad in the men's club that met monthly.

I learned a lot as I helped my dad move into his assisted-living community. One valuable lesson was that there often is room to negotiate your contract. For example, a few years after Dad moved into his building, his legs got weaker. This made his daily trip to the dining room, traveling down two long halls and multiple elevator rides, increasingly prohibitive. He expressed some concern about it, and even told me he was considering moving because of it. So we visited another assisted-living facility nearby. They courted us by serving a good meal and even offered us two freshly baked pies.

Next I set up a meeting with the administrators at Dad's current place. Dad was there too. I explained the reason he was contemplating a move. They asked me what they could do to persuade him to stay.

"Could Dad move into an apartment that's closer to the elevator?" I asked. "That would give him easier access to the dining room and exercise area." I also requested a rent decrease, a freeze on future rent increases for an additional year, free laundry done on a weekly basis, *and* that they assist him with the move at no cost.

To the amazement of both my dad and me, they agreed to everything.

Later Dad would joke, "The last thing I think about before I go to bed at night is the extra money that's in my pocket, not theirs."

My suggestion? Test the waters when you're looking at assisted-living options for your parents. It certainly doesn't hurt to ask if there are ways you can reduce your costs or get additional necessary services for little or no money. Ask questions, and explore all your options.

Chapter 7

Life in Dad's Pad and an Unexpected Illness

Assessing Life at Home and the Caretaking Team

As the months went by, I could see that age was really taking its toll on Dad. He was ninety years old. When I'd come by to visit him in his "pad," as he called it, I'd often find him sitting about a foot away from his flat-screen TV. He'd be using his remote to flip through the channels with the volume turned up so high I could only pray that his neighbors were equally deaf. He wouldn't hear me come in, so I'd gently tap him on the shoulder and give him a kiss. And he'd smile warmly at me and say, "It's good to see you."

Dad often appeared somewhat disheveled, with clothes that were torn, stained, or missing buttons. But his gray hair, or his "coiffure" as he called it, remained a focus of his attention. It was always neatly combed and cut.

In his apartment were piles and piles of napkins that he'd been taking from the dining room. "You never know when you'll need a napkin," he'd tell me. "I learned that from the Depression." He wouldn't let me throw any of them out.

Also strewn around the apartment were his clothes, draped over chairs; and newspapers were everywhere. It didn't bother him, but to me it was clearly a signal that we were closer to losing him on many levels. This disorderly clutter happened in spite of the fact that a woman came in weekly to clean his apartment. Except for keeping his hair immaculate, Dad just wasn't aware of either his appearance or his environment.

It made my siblings and me sad to see him living like that. We'd gently bring it to his attention in the hope of getting him to see that it was a problem. But Dad was fine with it, even when we'd have to push things aside to find a place to sit. What was even worse, his short-term memory began to go. We stopped mentioning it, because it would only get Dad upset. Testily, he'd remind us that he could dress and keep his apartment any way he wanted to. "That's what happens when you get old," he'd say.

My weekly ritual when I visited would include throwing out old newspapers, sorting mail, checking his prescriptions to see if they needed filling, and changing the battery in his hearing aids.

Dad began to forget to shave. One time I saw him trying to shave with his electric razor, but he didn't realize it wasn't turned on. Another time he forgot to plug it in so it could charge. I fixed it for him and in an unusual moment of self-reflection he said, "I used to be able to build anything I wanted to, and now I can't even figure out how to recharge my razor." He proudly reminisced about how he wired and built the basement of our home. After that I began to shave him.

I asked Dad if he was depressed. His answer revealed so much about the kind of man he was. He told me, "I'm not depressed. Just realistic about what my abilities and limitations are, which is why I appreciate your help so much when I need it."

In turn, I appreciated his gratitude, but it wasn't needed. I just wanted to keep him safe and independent. During my visits after that, I offered to buy him new clothes or mend the old ones. He wouldn't agree to it. As a child of the Depression he saw no reason to throw anything out until it literally disintegrated in his hands. Susie and I chose not to argue, realizing that this wasn't the best time to make a stand. We knew that more significant challenges would inevitably come.

One time Susie distracted Dad by engaging him in conversation, and I slipped into his bedroom. I grabbed some of his more ragged and worn items, then snuck out of his apartment and went to the garbage chute, where I thrust them in, then stood listening to them tumble, bouncing off the ducts, finally landing on the bottom, eleven floors down, with quite a thud. I stood there thinking about the man I knew when I was growing up. He'd been very fastidious about his appearance and his personal hygiene. I remember a couple of times when we'd all get dressed up for a special occasion and my parents would have us stand in front of a mirror. Dad would smile broadly. "What a good-looking family we are," he'd comment proudly, "and I only say it because it's true."

It's important to remind ourselves that the people we see in their old age today are an altered reflection of who they were when they were young. It can be hard to remember that when we're in the midst of all of the challenges aging creates and being a caretaker presents.

My dad was proud of saying he was a creature of habit, and he really was. As you may have guessed by reading his life story so far, he was not an adventurous, spontaneous guy. He took the same cruise-ship vacation six times in a row, because he didn't like surprises when traveling. He liked knowing what to expect. "I am not a pioneer" was one of his favorite sayings. He wore the same clothes for over thirty years. I knew exactly where he was at any given moment of the day or night, which in retrospect was a source of comfort for me. If I came to visit or called and he wasn't where I thought he should be, I would worry that something was wrong. It did help that the staff in his building were great about letting me know if they had seen him. This was very reassuring for me.

In fact, Dad really was pretty set in his ways after over ninety years of life. We were all incredibly blessed that his health was so good for such a long time. My siblings and I were very grateful for how Dad took pride in his independence. He liked controlling his life and his routines; he only asked for help when he felt it was necessary. We were lulled into thinking that he'd reach a milestone hundred years without any problems.

As I describe in the introduction, Dad took a fall when he was ninety. I did take him to the doctor in spite of his mild protests. I'd been a bit concerned because even prior to the fall I had noticed he seemed to be increasingly confused. He was also more disheveled than usual. His ability to walk and his balance appeared worse as well. Plus, he had no awareness of this, in itself a symptom that caused me great concern.

The doctor did a thorough examination on my dad. Insisting that he had no memory problems, Dad gave incorrect responses to the doctor's questions, while all along I stood behind him, signaling the correct answers. I'd known this doctor for over thirty years. He specialized in working with elderly people. And he understood that my responses were more reliable than my dad's.

He asked Dad to take off his shirt so he could examine him further. I noticed that Dad had a watch on his wrist and another near his elbow.

"Why are you wearing two watches?" I asked him.

Dad looked very surprised. "How the hell did that get there? I've been looking for that watch for two weeks. Thanks, you helped me find it. This alone makes it a good idea we came here."

I looked at the doctor and this sadly confirmed my fears about Dad's confusion and memory problems.

The doctor told us to head over to the emergency room immediately so that Dad could get an MRI. He wanted some sharply defined pictures to get a closer look at what was going on in Dad's brain. It was imperative, he told us, to find out what was happening as quickly as possible.

I took Dad to the hospital where I'd worked for almost a decade, because I knew he would get excellent care there. I'd been a social worker on their rehab unit, working with many elderly people who had strokes or neurological problems.

Sitting next to Dad as he was placed in the MRI chamber, I wondered what we should expect to find. An MRI machine looks like a large, long tube with a hole in the center. It's designed so that a person can lie down on a metal bed that slowly slides into the center of it. As the pictures are being taken, the machine makes a loud banging noise. I had sat with my mom for an MRI, and she had told me it felt like a casket. So beforehand I warned Dad that taking the MRI would be uncomfortable because it was a very loud and confined space. He assured me that it wouldn't bother him. He had also taken Mom for this test and was familiar with it. This was not our family's first experience with serious health problems.

I carefully watched my dad. I also watched the technician who could be seen through the glass window outside our room. I knew that if she were to contact a radiologist or the internist during the MRI, that could mean there was a problem.

She made a call.

I came out to speak with her privately and asked, "Did you find a bleeder or a tumor?"

"How did you know?" she replied in surprise. "I'm not supposed to say anything."

I explained that I'd worked at the hospital. Reluctantly she told me that the MRI had revealed there was bleeding in my dad's brain. I went and explained this to Dad. He didn't have his hearing aids, so it was difficult to be certain he understood every aspect of what was going on.

They immediately moved Dad back to the ER where he could be examined by a physician—having earlier been seen quickly by a nurse and a resident—and get a more comprehensive workup. I was struck by how calm he remained each step of the way. He trusted me enough to just follow my instructions without any protest or complaints.

It was unsettling how quickly things could change. I knew he was most certainly facing a major health crisis. We both sat quietly while a nurse took Dad's vital signs. A resident came in to test his reflexes, vision, memory, and orientation as to where he was. Then she told me that the neurosurgeon was on the phone in the nurses' ER station and wanted to speak with me.

Quickly I went to the nurses' station and picked up the phone. The neurosurgeon confirmed that Dad had a cerebral hemorrhage. The only option for treatment was to drill a hole in his skull so they could go in and repair the damage. However, the neurosurgeon told me that he was very reluctant to do this type of surgery on a ninety-year-old man.

"You haven't met my father yet," I replied.

We agreed it should be Dad's decision to make. I asked the doctor to more fully describe the procedure and to candidly detail both the risks and the reasons Dad needed to have it. If the surgery wasn't done quickly, he told me, Dad was at risk of dying from the continued bleeding in his brain. I told the doctor I would share the information with my dad. Whatever he decided would be the course of action we would pursue.

So I relayed to Dad everything the neurosurgeon had told me.

Dad just looked at me and laughed. "Once that bullet missed my head in World War II, everything else has been gravy. Let's go ahead and do this."

Twenty minutes later, we were off to the intensive-care unit.

Frankly, I was in a somewhat stunned state. If we hadn't gone to the doctor, there was a good chance my dad would have died. At least this surgery offered him a better chance of survival, even with the risks. It all seemed quite surreal how quickly it happened. Everything felt changed as I looked around at all the equipment in the ICU.

Dad, on the other hand, was totally relaxed and unafraid. It was genuine. I was in awe of his courage given the information he had just received. He immediately began joking and flirting with the nurses.

A little while later, I asked him how he was doing.

"I've lived a great life and feel very lucky," he replied. "Whatever happens with this surgery will happen."

I called my siblings to share the news with them. Susie was nearby and could come, but Caryn was in London and Danny was in California. They would stay in touch by phone to see if they needed to come.

The next day Dad went into surgery. Susie was there with me. Dad was groggy but calm as we kissed him on his forehead before they wheeled him away. All we could do was wait. The surgery took longer than we thought it would.

With each passing minute we became more concerned. Finally, after several hours, the neurosurgeon appeared. He told us that he was able to repair the bleed, and that Dad did great. He was waiting in the recovery room and was medically stable.

When they wheeled Dad back into his ICU room, Susie and I were right there with him, and took our seats by his bed. He had the usual IVs attached to his arm. He looked very frail as he lay there. I thought about his perseverance during World War II. And he had been incredibly strong in his work, which demanded he repeatedly lift very heavy weights. We hoped the tenacity he had shown in his younger years would rise up now to help him heal and recover. He needed that strength to face the challenges that would await him in the days ahead.

I recalled being at the bedside of the hundreds of elderly patients I had worked with. I knew that the hospital staff had many patients' care needs to balance and little extra time. In Dad they would just see the shell of an elderly, sick person, silently assessing all the things he was now unable to do, possibly thinking about the care plan that must be created and implemented.

With these elderly patients, there was no evidence left to show their youth, their vibrancy, their rich life histories. No way to know how they tackled the challenges they faced in the days prior to their hospital stays. The initial images and impressions we had never told the whole life story of the person helplessly facing us. I thought about that as the nurse looked down on my dad in his hospital bed. She adjusted his intravenous lines and took his blood pressure and heart rate. My dad's story would be unknown to the staff unless we chose to share some of our family stories. And I knew I wanted them to know more about him as a person; I hoped they would take better care of him because of this.

I knew that Dad was going to need rehabilitation to help him regain his balance and his ability to walk, as well as to improve his ability to dress and bathe himself. The first step would be a thorough evaluation to correctly assess what he could do and his limitations. I contacted a doctor with whom I'd worked on the rehab floor. She was wonderful. She agreed to come and assess Dad to determine if he would be a candidate for rehab.

She examined him to see if he could answer simple questions and understand commands, like "Lift your right leg." She looked at the range of motion and strength in his arms and legs. When she told me she would like to transfer him to the rehab area, I was incredibly grateful because I knew the only other alternative would be to have him transferred to a nursing home.

I understood how grueling rehabilitation treatment would be, and I wanted to warn Dad about it. I explained it would feel like he was running a marathon multiple times a day. That was the analogy I had used with my own patients. It was an indication of the hard work he'd have to be doing in order to get himself well enough to return to his apartment.

Rehab involves physical, occupational, and speech therapies. Each therapist came in to evaluate Dad's level of function and the rehab doctor let me observe his initial assessments.

Although his speech was perfectly all right, he had other, extreme deficits. The speech therapist asked him to draw a picture of a clock showing three o'clock. He drew a half circle with several numbers bunched up in the right corner and pointed one hand of the clock on a three. He had no awareness that what he'd drawn was incorrect. I thought about the ramifications of this. He couldn't write checks. He couldn't read bills or bank statements, pre-scriptions, or menus. He couldn't read anything accurately right now.

In addition, Dad needed help standing up. At first, he was unable to walk more than a short distance without help from a nurse or a therapist. He also required a walker to help him move and maintain his balance. In order to return safely to his assisted-living apartment, he'd need—at a min-imum—to be able to walk twice a day from his apartment to the elevator and to the dining room. Thank goodness I discussed these distances with the physical therapist, so we had a specific goal to work toward.

The occupational therapist's goal was to help Dad be able to dress himself, and to get himself in and out of his bathtub/shower stall. I had arranged for him to get a shower bench to sit on, and had also ordered him a walker. Because of my social work experience I knew that all these therapies and these assistive devices would be covered by Medicare. The doctor and therapists needed to order them; they could document the medical necessity.

Dad was a great patient. He was motivated to get out of the hospital, and he worked hard. He listened and learned from his nurses and therapists, who were amazed by his progress. After only a couple of weeks, Dad was able to "graduate" and go back home, which felt miraculous to us.

Once he was back, I met with the head of nursing and the therapists who worked there to give them his medical records. I shared information as to what the rehab doctor and the hospital therapists had recommended for his continued goals.

At this point, by continuing to use his walker, Dad was able to walk the necessary distance to get to the dining room without anyone helping him. We arranged for the therapists in his building to continue to work with him. The physical therapist helped him to walk farther distances. Eventually he was able to just use a cane for additional support.

Dad was also assessed by the facility's occupational therapist and was deemed safe to take a bath and dress independently without help. He didn't cook so that was not a problem.

For a few years after his brain surgery, Dad functioned pretty well and remained fairly independent. However, we began to notice the issues with his hygiene and balance again, and we felt renewed concern about his safety. He was ninety-four at this point. We also were seeing that he needed to use the bathroom much more frequently. And a new problem emerged. He wasn't always able to get there in a timely way. This caused him to have episodes of urinary incontinence. We got concerned about his skin breaking down and his not being clean. It was clear that he needed additional help.

We were very glad that his facility offered support services; we could hire an aide to come in as many times a day as we requested. We wanted the aide there to make sure that

Dad went to the bathroom safely and frequently. Regarding the financial aspect of this service, I knew Medicare wouldn't cover the cost, and I also knew that Dad would never agree to pay for it.

My siblings and I were clear that we wanted to have the comfort of knowing that Dad was safe and clean. So I met with the head nurse and we devised a plan for an aide to check in on Dad three times a day. The aide would also help Dad with bathing, and make sure that he changed his clothes as necessary. There would also be someone to do his laundry for him.

Danny, Caryn, Susie, and I agreed to share the costs for these services. We felt extremely fortunate that we had the financial resources to make it happen, and we were also very grateful for the staff who worked with us as a team.

I simply told Dad that the staff wanted to stop in and check on him because they liked him and thought he was such a good guy. He thought that was great.

Assessing Life at Home and the Caretaking Team

Once we leave our parents' home, all bets are off. By this I mean that they choose to live the way they want to. Even in our role as their adult children, with loving relationships in place, we may find that our parents often don't welcome our input about how they manage their home or their day-to-day lives. They may become very set in their routine; that familiarity often is a source of comfort to them. It also represents their independence, their beliefs, and their lifestyle.

When you visit your aging parents, there are warning signs to watch out for, indicating that they may need additional help—even if they are not aware of it. In her book *The Eldercare Handbook*, Stella Mora Henry mentions some of these important warning signs:

- Are there buttons missing from your parent's clothing?

- Is your parent's clothing unkempt or unclean?

- Does she wear the same clothes day after day?

- Is there body odor?

- Does it look as if your parent is not brushing her teeth regularly?

- Has your mother stopped caring about her hair and makeup?

- Has your father stopped shaving and getting regular trims?

Henry also describes the behaviors that may indicate a deterioration in your senior's ability to function.

Personal Care

Deteriorated personal hygiene, uncombed hair, soiled clothing, mismatched clothing, difficulty getting in and out of tub or shower without assistance, infrequent bathing, incontinence.

Housekeeping

Accumulation of garbage or spoiled food, stained carpets, piles of dirty laundry, unclean silverware, sticky kitchen counter, reluctance to accept help.

Meals and Appetite

Difficulty preparing meals, decreased appetite, noticeable weight loss or gain, stale food, empty refrigerator.

Memory

Forgetting appointments and names, repeating stories in conversation, regularly losing or misplacing objects, loss of recent memory, repeated phone calls for the same reason, forgetting how to use the telephone.

Communication

Difficulty finding specific words, increasingly illegible handwriting, difficulty learning or retaining new information.

Mobility

Slower pace when walking, difficulty climbing stairs, unsteady gait, frequent falls, balance problems.

Depression

Unexplainable anxiety or irritability, decreased interest in family or friends, avoidance of previously enjoyed activities.

Medication

Frequently missed daily medications, difficulty recalling if medication was taken, overuse of medication, untimely reordering of medication.

Finances

Unopened mail, unpaid bills, or bills paid twice, unbalanced or overdrawn checkbook, unexplained credit card charges, frequent transfers from savings into checking accounts, threatening letters from collection agencies.

Driving

Unsafe driving speed, difficulty negotiating turns, unexplained dents or scrapes, increased traffic violations, difficulty parking.

So if these red flags appear, how do you handle it? It can be a delicate dance when you begin the discussion, outlining your observations and your concerns. Keep in mind that what you see may not be what *they* see. Denial can be a way of helping them to cope with anxiety and fear.

Be sure to frame this conversation in terms of your love and concern for them. Starting out by pointing out all the problems you're observing may cause your aging loved ones to assume a defensive or angry stance. All they'll be able to hear may be what feels like criticism or judgments from you.

Think ahead of time as to what might be the most effective way to approach them. In some families, for example, there may be an individual who could be a spokesperson for all the adult siblings, so that your parents won't feel "ganged up on." Or you may want to organize a family meeting so that parents and siblings can explore this territory together.

In their book *Caring for Your Parents,* Delehanty and Ginzler address this issue, offering suggestions and possible scenarios to help you get your message across in a loving and supportive manner.

Be direct and show your concerns. Especially if your parent seems resistant or reluctant, you may need to raise an issue your parent would like to avoid. Don't be confrontational. Instead use "I" messages. Tell how you are feeling, not what they need to do. Remember you are in this together. "Dad, I am really worried about you falling on the stairs. You have tripped a couple of times. How can I help keep you safe?" Be ready to be "found out." You've tried to be subtle

or indirect, and they've seen right through
you. Laugh at yourself. It could turn out to be
the perfect opening: "Yea, okay. So much for
subtlety. I'm so bad at this stuff. But it's been
on my mind, and I really think we need to start
talking about it."

Many people have found it helps to write a
letter to their parents, even if they live nearby.
Sometimes it is easier to express in writing what is
difficult to say or what older parents resist hearing.
If all efforts hit a brick wall and the direct talk just
isn't happening, don't hesitate to seek support in the
community.

If there simply aren't any relatives who have a good
relationship with your aging loved one, another option
might be to elicit the help of clergy or a trusted friend to
initiate this dialogue. The key is to get someone your loved
one trusts and whose opinion she values.

Creating an Open Dialogue with Your Parents

If you're organizing a family meeting, there are several
things to consider. Whom do you want to participate?
Scheduling can be a challenge if there are siblings who live
elsewhere. You can include them by using Internet options

like Skype or FaceTime, or by setting up a telephone conference call. Keep in mind, though, that including *too* many people could make it difficult for your parents to follow the conversation.

In *Caring for Your Parents*, Delehanty and Ginzler offer these recommendations for the family meeting:

> *Starting out the goal is raising issues, not necessarily finding solutions. The most critical aspect of bringing up the subject is getting all the concerns on the table. You might consider drawing a list of questions before the meeting so your parents and the rest of the people involved can think about what they want and how they feel. You can and should gather some information—regarding resources in the community about such issues as Medicare, advance directives, living arrangements—but only to encourage the thought process, not necessarily to come up with definitive answers.*

Have someone take notes throughout the meeting, or record it, so there will be no confusion about who said what. This information can then be shared with those who couldn't participate. It can also be easily referenced later.

By the end of the meeting, you should have a list of the areas where your parent will need some type of support. Identify people who can assist with these items. In some cases it might be a family member. Sometimes it might be a neighbor, community program, or health-care professional. Also take a look at the frequency with which these interventions might be needed. All family members should have an equal opportunity to participate in this discussion if appropriate.

Before the first meeting is over, people should agree on a time frame when a follow-up meeting will be held. The goal of this next meeting is to assess how successful these interventions are. Are the caretakers working out well? Are there gaps in care? Give your parents and other participants a chance to discuss any concerns or problems that may have arisen. Don't allow too much time to pass before this follow-up meeting is held or you may lose some of the momentum that was initiated by putting this care plan in place.

If it seems to you that the care plan is not succeeding, try to come to this next meeting with some additional resources and information. This can include info about more intensive and extensive care options, such as assisted living, a full-time live-in caretaker, or a nursing home if necessary.

If you're finding yourself surprised or daunted by this role reversal, in which you're attending family meetings talking about taking on the role of caretaker for your parents, keep in mind that you're a product of all of your past relationships and roles that evolved from the time you were a child growing up in your family. This all influences the relationships you have today. You may have family scattered in different states or different countries. There may be a sibling or close relative who lives nearby but cannot handle all—or any—of the necessary caretaking responsibilities.

Regardless of the current health of your parents, I encourage you to spend some time thinking about the type of assistance you would be willing and able to offer if they were unable to take care of themselves anymore. A variety of obstacles and challenges can appear when adult children are faced with the prospect of becoming a caretaker for a parent:

- It can be difficult to maintain a balance between caretaking responsibilities and your commitment to your work and your immediate family.

- Different careers make different demands in terms of time, stress, and travel.

- Barriers can exist, created by old sibling/family relationships, labels, and dynamics that remained in place as you grew into adulthood.

- Your personal life may have financial and time pressures.

- You and your siblings may have made different choices about where you decided to live and build your own life.

- Your individual relationship with your parents is unique to you and may differ greatly from that of your siblings or other relatives.

- You may relate differently to your parents than your siblings do.

- Your current relationship with your parents was greatly influenced by the parenting messages they gave you when you were growing up. If you grew up in an abusive home, you will likely feel less inclined to help your parents in later life than someone who grew up in a loving home with parents modeling the importance of family relationships.

This can be a long and challenging process. Approach it with as much patience as you can. If you try something and it doesn't work, please don't give up. Hopefully, all parties are willing to exert themselves to thoughtfully analyze the current situation and come up with the best way to all work together in order to be effective caretakers for your elderly loved ones.

Chapter 8

No Mas

Dad continued to do pretty well after his surgery. But as I mentioned in the previous chapter, we began to have concerns about his ability to take care of himself, and managed to bring in help from the facility. That was a comfort.

Another concern for us was that Dad's hearing got progressively worse. When he was ninety he'd gotten state-of-the art hearing aids and I'd been thrilled by how much they helped. When he'd had his old hearing aids, Dad had been adept with them. He was so good at it, in fact, that sometimes he would purposely turn them off and not tell us. This gave him the power to just tune us out when he felt like it. (It was an old trick he'd used with Mom when she was ill and had become verbally abusive with him.) It was a game he liked to play. But this game wasn't fun for us. We were very concerned about his safety. He wouldn't hear the phone ring, which made it challenging for us to communicate with him. Also, the daily safety checks that his facility offered weren't successful when he didn't answer his phone because he couldn't hear it.

I knew from my research that people's senses decline as they age. Articles I'd read recommended that people need to be proactive about compensating for their deficits. Dad was very impressed with his new hearing aids. They were programmed to work together to amplify and clarify sound, even on the telephone.

One night I kept trying to call Dad and the line was busy. I figured he had accidentally knocked his phone off the hook. I called the concierge at his facility, and asked them to check on my dad and put the phone back on the hook. Dad's schedule was entirely predictable. He never deviated from it. It was 6:30 P.M.; he always went to bed at 6:00 P.M., so that's where he should have been.

The concierge called me to say that Dad wasn't in his apartment. The phone *had* been off the hook, and they replaced it.

"Are you *sure* he's not there?" I asked.

"We looked in his apartment, and he was gone."

I was very worried. It was a cold, rainy night, and I couldn't imagine Dad going out.

The other big concern was they were upgrading the elevators in his building, which meant that service was often slow. Dad had become impatient waiting for the elevator. He'd recently told me he was using the stairwell to go to meals. These stairs were back stairs and primarily used as a fire escape. He had to go down *eleven* flights. I had asked him to stop doing this. I was fearful he would fall and nobody would find him.

"Please have your security team check the stairs," I told the concierge. That was the only other place I could think of where Dad might have gone.

She called me back. They hadn't found anyone on the stairs.

I was really beginning to panic. I called Susie. She immediately wanted to call the police.

"I'm going to check his apartment first," I told her. "I want to see if I can find his wallet, cane, or walker— anything that might give us a clue as to where he's gone."

If necessary I would drive up and down the streets of his neighborhood. What if he was confused, or if he'd fallen and couldn't get help? As I drove toward his apartment, I was imagining all the things that might have gone wrong. Just before I got there, I got a call on my cell phone from the concierge.

"We found him," she told me, "and he's all right."

"Where was he?" I asked with relief.

"He was in his bed, sleeping."

I was astounded. How could that be? I wanted to scream.

The telephone the security guard had put back on the hook was in Dad's bedroom, less than five feet from his bed. How could that person have been unaware that my father was asleep in his bed?

Dad felt terrible about worrying Susie and me. I assured him it was not his fault. But this incident reinforced my conviction that better communication was extremely important.

I decided that the combination of a good hearing aid and

a phone with extra amplification would be a smart first step. I did some research about programs for those with impaired hearing, and found one that offered state-of-the-art amplified telephones for free. I also contacted the phone company to see what information they had on this topic. And while searching on the Internet for phones for the hearing-impaired in my area, I found some interesting possibilities. I discovered a state-funded program. We just had to present a letter from Dad's audiologist about his hearing deficits.

This phone system worked well for a while, until Dad got tired of using his hearing aids. This happened often when he was sitting in his apartment. Our shouting conversations began again. I found myself screaming into the phone at times, loudly spelling words. It became an exercise in frustration. It finally got so bad I would have to drive to his apartment to have a face- to-face conversation regarding any information I had to relay.

I again jumped on the Internet to learn about telephone communication options. I found some companies that make a telephone that has what looks like a small computer screen. It's a captioned telephone. This device is similar to the captions we see on TV. When a person receives a phone call, everything the caller says can be read on the screen. It "types" as the caller talks. The technology is similar to the voice-recognition technology used with cell phones or other transcription devices, like Dragon NaturallySpeaking. With a captioned telephone, the responses from the person receiving the call are also typed out so they can be read. Even voice messages are displayed.

The important thing I learned about this device is that

it works through a router. It can be installed by a cable company or, if you have Wi-Fi set up in your parent's home, you can do it yourself, but there must be a wireless local network available for it to work.

Dad was still an avid reader so he felt quite comfortable with this medium. However, it took him a while to figure out how to work his new phone as it's sort of like a minicomputer. I needed to give him repeated lessons. We also wrote down the instructions for him. The good news was that it definitely worked better than our old system of relying on Dad's hearing aids.

One of the reasons I believe my dad had done so well physically throughout his life was that he continued to make time for exercise and staying active. He rode a stationary bike, walked on a treadmill, and spent time outdoors in the sunlight. This exercise improved his endurance, his balance, his leg strength, and breathing. It was great for his cardiovascular health. And I also believe the physical exercise also helped him feel better about himself. He was proud that his weight hadn't changed even into his eighties and nineties.

Dad also kept his mind active by reading and by doing crossword puzzles every day. If he stopped doing any of these activities, it was an immediate indicator that something was wrong with him. It helped us be proactive regarding his health.

This went on from the time my dad was ninety until he was ninety-six. And for much of the time, he was content simply watching TV and resting. He enjoyed his daily shot of Canadian Club and his Milky Way or Snickers bar. He also had a sundae every night after dinner. The highlight of his day remained carefully studying the menu and making his way to the dining room to eat.

When I visited him in his apartment, I always found his daily menus. He would circle items and make notes on multiple menus from the same day so that he was prepared when he got to the dining room.

As I mentioned earlier, we had to encourage him to use his cane as he walked. He was reluctant to use it; he didn't want to publicly appear to be incapacitated in any way. All in all, though, he seemed pretty content.

His standard response when asked how he was doing was, "As well as can be expected." We never heard any complaints from him. Little things, like a phone call from us kids or a kind word from the staff, made him very happy.

But we still had considerable concern about his ability to safely walk. It was clear to us that walking was becoming more challenging. After repeated questioning, Dad would reluctantly reveal that his legs felt weaker and stiffer. He still would go for his workouts in the gym. But he wasn't able to do as much.

The only medication Dad was on at age ninety-six was a B12 shot, and a blood-pressure medication he started taking after his cerebral hemorrhage. The facility's nurse would come once a month to give him his shot. She told me that all she had to do was knock on his door. When she opened it, he knew why she was there. "He smiles and drops his pants," she said, laughing.

I had begun to notice that Dad's short-term memory was getting worse. For example, he forgot conversations we'd just had. Before I picked him up for a dentist appointment, I'd have to call him. When I'd ask him about these lapses in memory, he would just say, "That's what happens when you get older."

In September of 2013, during the Jewish high holidays, I was visiting Dad and he commented on the cantor who had been singing all night long. "He still is singing. Can you hear him?" Dad asked me. "He has such a beautiful voice."

I paused and listened, desperately hoping to hear something besides the silence.

Later, I contacted Dad's doctor. "Should we be concerned about this auditory hallucination?" I asked.

"Was he *enjoying* the singing?"

"Yes, he was."

"Don't worry then," the doctor told me. "It's not harming him. And there's not much you can do."

I knew he was right.

Were there times when I'd thought about my dad dying? Of course there were. In a way, though, he also seemed invincible to me, and to my siblings too. But when I imagined how he would die, I assumed it would be in his sleep or possibly a heart attack. As I look back, I realize that was simply how I'd *hoped* it would be. I wanted it to be quick and painless for him. It was both an unselfish hope for him, and, frankly, a selfish one for our family.

Dad had surprised us all with his recovery from brain surgery and his ability to resume his normal routine. It seemed that all he needed was the additional supervision and help from his aides to maintain his personal hygiene and safety.

He was doing so well that Susie and I had decided to

go to Greece to celebrate my sixtieth birthday. We would be gone for two weeks, and my niece, Blythe, agreed to check in with him while we were gone. This would be the first time in thirty years that Susie and I would be away at the same time. But we felt that with the supervision from Dad's facility along with the support of my niece, he'd be fine.

A week after we left, however, Dad was admitted to the hospital. While trying to swallow his food, it instead traveled to his lungs, and he developed pneumonia. Such a small trigger caused a major problem.

While Dad was in the hospital the doctors learned that his heart wasn't beating at a normal rate. This is not unusual with elderly people: when treating one ailment, doctors commonly find some additional medical problem. In Dad's case, his heart would occasionally stop beating for as long as three seconds. They told us that a decision about a pacemaker should be made quickly. Our family was now under pressure to make a difficult decision.

Meanwhile, although his pneumonia had successfully been treated, Dad began having episodes of confusion and also became uncharacteristically angry and agitated. He didn't always recognize familiar faces. He was uncertain about the time and day. The hospital's speech therapist also learned that his ability to swallow had deteriorated. He could no longer drink thin liquids or eat the food he had always eaten. He was only allowed food that was "nectar thick." Anything thinner than tomato juice was prohibited. This meant that Dad required supervision during all meals. Eating had to be done slowly, or he would risk getting pneumonia again and possibly dying.

Far away in Greece, Susie and I were stunned when we got the first e-mail about Dad's sudden change in health. We would get subsequent calls from Blythe at 1:30 A.M. and 4:00 A.M. Feelings of anxiety, guilt, and helplessness weighed heavily on us. Being so far away at a time when he needed us most was frightening. We continued to monitor our cell phones and e-mail, desperate for any new information. From the moment we got the news, our thoughts focused on our dad. What could we do to help him get through this unexpected crisis? We thought about cutting our trip short. But my husband, Steve, and Blythe advised us that Dad was medically stable for now; although his condition was serious, it wasn't life-threatening. And Danny told us he was going to Chicago to stay with Dad until we got back. I knew his visit with our dad was important for them both. And it was a comfort for Susie and me, knowing he was there. We were staying in touch with Caryn by phone and by e-mail, so that we were all kept up-to-date on what was happening.

After Dad was admitted to the hospital, Steve and Blythe were there constantly advocating for him. They communicated with the doctors and basically lived at the hospital. Dad nicknamed Steve "the diplomat" because he had to frequently intervene on his behalf. Blythe was eight months pregnant. We were concerned that the stress would have a negative impact on both her and the baby.

And then another health problem emerged for Dad. Even when he didn't have to urinate, he felt the need to empty his bladder. Conversely, there were also times when he couldn't urinate when he *did* need to go. The doctors discovered that he had an enlarged prostate, so he needed a catheter to help him with this.

Finally, Susie and I flew back to Chicago, landing at 11:00 P.M. We went directly from the airport to the hospital. At the time, Susie was quite sick with terrible congestion; she also had an immobilized arm as a result of a bad fall our last morning in Greece. We learned later that she had pneumonia.

The doctors were pressing us to make a decision about the pacemaker. Danny, Steve, and Blythe hadn't felt comfortable making this critical decision without input from Susie and me, and I strongly believed we needed to first see Dad. I wanted to assess his condition and level of awareness before determining what the next step should be.

Not sure what to expect, Susie and I went to Dad's hospital room. We walked in with a mixture of fatigue, fear, and relief at finally being with him. Based on the reports we'd been receiving, I wasn't sure if he would recognize us. We'd been told, "He's been seeing cows outside of his room." The cow turned out to be a machine hanging from a crane that looked like it had horns coming out of it. It explained that bizarre comment, at least.

Dad smiled warmly at us. "How was your trip to Greece?" he asked.

"It was okay," I answered briefly, wanting to focus the conversation on him. "How do you feel?"

"As well as can be expected."

Dad noticed that Susie was wearing a medical mask, and hanging back because she didn't want to risk sharing her germs with him. "You look worse than I do," he said. "Are you okay?"

What a relief to see him so oriented! He seemed his old self—more concerned about us than he was about his own problems.

The staff had told us that Dad had "sundowner's syndrome," which is a condition that occurs in the early evening hours and into the night. Sufferers feel confused, disoriented, and sometimes agitated. There was no evidence of it when we saw him that night. He smiled at us. He was sharp, alert, and clearly happy to see us. I asked him some questions in order to assess his level of understanding regarding his medical condition. His responses confirmed that he understood what the doctors had told him, and why he was in the hospital. We talked about the pacemaker, and its risks and its benefits.

"I'm not afraid of the risks, and I don't want to give up," he said firmly.

The next day, Susie, Danny, and I—with Caryn's blessing from afar—discussed the question together. It was not an easy one. Danny expressed fears about Dad's quality of life. He'd seen Dad at his worst: confused, agitated, needing round-the-clock care, and unable to eat solid foods. We knew that the decision could mean life or death for our dad. Without the pacemaker, Dad's lifespan would be shortened. Ultimately, we felt we needed to respect his wishes, and arranged for him to have the pacemaker inserted the next day.

I was with Dad as he went in for the pacemaker procedure.

The doctor had assured me she'd performed this surgery numerous times on patients even older than my dad. It was a relatively easy surgery to do, she said, with few risks. And Dad tolerated the surgery very well. After a few hours he was back in his hospital room, tired but in good spirits.

But that night, his recovery didn't go smoothly. He'd gotten considerably weaker having been confined to a hospital bed for over a week. At night, he experienced confusion so extensive that a few times they had to tie his hands to the bed rails. He kept trying to grab his catheter and pull it out. The damage caused by pulling out his catheter included serious blood loss and internal damage. This resulted in a great deal of pain. And it also made it difficult for even the expert urologists to reinsert his catheter.

It was heartbreaking for our family to have him beg us to remove his restraints. He had no memory of his confusion or his attempts to remove his catheter. He felt like he was being treated like a caged animal.

Finally, having been at the hospital all day, I was beyond exhausted, and left. But a few minutes later I got a call from a nurse at the hospital, asking me to return as Dad had gotten extremely agitated.

I rushed back to his room. He looked at me and said, "Iris, do you have a knife with you?"

"Why do you need a knife?" I responded, my heart sinking.

"I need to cut these ropes off my hands."

"I can't do that, Dad, for your own safety."

"You're either with me or against me," he answered angrily, "and apparently you've chosen to be against me. That's okay, because I'll do this on my own, without your help." He began trying to grab at the ties attached to his restraints. The staff couldn't give him any more sedatives because in his weakened condition it was not safe.

I cried all the way home.

This was the first time in my life that Dad had ever believed I wasn't there for him. There was nothing I could do to make him understand I was only trying to protect him.

When I went back to Dad's room the next morning, I was guilt-ridden and anxious. Luckily he had no recollection of the night before or what had transpired between us. I convinced the staff to take off his restraints while I was there. I promised them I would watch him carefully. Thankfully, that plan worked for all of us.

For the next three months our lives were an emotional roller-coaster ride.

Things started going on a downhill slant when I walked into Dad's hospital room and found a large cup of water and ice at his bedside table, even though he was not allowed to drink water. Drinking that water could kill him. He could aspirate it, develop pneumonia, and die. I threw it in the trash, but day after day, I found a cup of water and ice in his room.

In deep frustration, I arranged for a meeting with the supervisor in charge of the staff on that unit. I asked him to put up a sign on the door of Dad's room, stating that he was only allowed to have thick liquids. The supervisor told me that wasn't possible. He said that state regulations forbade it.

"Would you prefer a lawsuit when my father dies due to your staff's repeated incompetence?" I said heatedly.

"I'm going to go out on a limb for you," he said, placatingly. He went to Dad's little closet, located in a far corner of the room. He opened the door, and taped a sign there with instructions for a thick liquid diet.

This was his idea of a huge concession.

There was no way that anyone would ever see that sign. I knew it and so did he.

A team of state inspectors happened to be on the unit while Dad was a patient there. I talked to Susie about going to them and letting them know how upset we were with the staff's unwillingness to work with us to ensure our father's safety. She was worried there would be retribution if I did. Reluctantly, I agreed not to say or do anything more.

It was incredibly difficult coping with Dad's medical decline. It seemed to us that unless we were almost superhumanly vigilant, he would be in a horribly vulnerable position. Every day, when Susie and I left the hospital, we worried that the people who were supposed to be taking care of him might inadvertently harm him. It kept us awake at night.

One morning, I accompanied Dad to a physical therapy session. Suddenly, while he was standing, his eyes glazed over. He was unable to focus. I went to get the therapist who immediately knew something was wrong. She had him sit down and quickly wrapped a pulse oximeter—a small sensor device that measures the oxygen level in the blood—around his finger. The device showed no reading. It wasn't working.

I quickly ran to get a nurse and to ask for another device. When I returned, Dad wasn't responding to anything the physical therapist said. The nurse came quickly and the pulse oximeter he had didn't register anything either. The information from that tiny device would give them instant data about what was wrong, so that they could respond appropriately. Neither device worked.

Just then, my dad became responsive again. He was able to follow the physical therapist's commands. He recognized me so I knew he was okay. But I was still stunned. I couldn't believe they didn't even have basic equipment that worked.

I lay awake at night, waiting for a phone call and a voice telling me that something had gone wrong or that my dad had died. During the days, while we were with Dad, we shielded him from our fears. He was totally unaware of the mistakes that were being made around him. Fortunately, there were nurses we did speak with who understood our concerns. They silently nodded their heads as if this wasn't the first time there had been a problem. They were very good with him, which was a comfort to us. We trusted them to take care of Dad.

Danny, Caryn, Susie, Steve, Blythe, and I discussed the possibility of transferring Dad to another hospital. This meant leaving doctors who knew him. We felt very comfortable with them. I also worried that a transfer would further confuse Dad and hinder his recovery. Neither option felt right.

During this time, we were also advocating for Dad to get not just physical therapy, but occupational therapy too. The combination of lying in a hospital bed for ten days and undergoing surgery had made him very weak. This was all complicated by his limited food intake. He had already dropped twenty pounds.

After a week, Dad was transferred to a rehab unit in the hospital at our urging. All our hopes about his ability to return home were tied to a successful stay there. After a week in the new unit, Dad became medically stable. This meant that he'd soon be discharged from the hospital. Our family had to be proactive by making a plan for where he would go. Dad had made it clear that he wanted to return to his apartment, and we felt we had to give him this opportunity. However, we'd need to see if he could manage, given the additional limitations on his ability to move and to eat. We all felt reluctant to consider a nursing home for him without trying this plan first.

One of the biggest challenges we faced was finding the right caretaker for Dad. That person had to be knowledgeable in catheter care and familiar with Dad's special diet. A major consideration was the caretaker's ability to get along with Dad.

As for Dad, he just wanted to be in his apartment again and get back to his routine. We were troubled to see that he still didn't understand that he would have ongoing difficulties with his mobility and diet. We knew he'd get frustrated that he couldn't simply return to the dining room and eat the food he relished.

We found a well-respected agency. They had companions on staff who could live with Dad, help him with his daily care, and ensure he ate the proper food. We met with the supervisor and a potential caregiver, who said he had lots of experience. It all sounded good, but unfortunately, things didn't go as planned.

One of the companions called me in a panic at one thirty in the morning to tell me that Dad had pulled out his catheter. He told me my dad's bedroom looked like a crime scene because of all the blood. I rushed over. When I got to his apartment I found the staff nurse there. She confirmed that Dad would need to be taken to the emergency room to have the catheter replaced by a doctor.

Over the next couple of weeks, Dad had to go back to the hospital three times and was also sent to the ER twice. He was pulling out his catheter. Another time he was left unattended by his caretaker and fell. At one point, his blood loss was so severe the doctors were talking about giving him transfusions.

Three hours after Dad had been discharged from the hospital for the third time, I got a call from his companion, who told me that Dad had been readmitted after pulling his catheter out yet again. The companion had called for an ambulance to take him to the hospital. I told him I would meet them there.

The situation was so bad, I never turned my phone off. I would lie awake in bed, waiting for the inevitable next phone call. It was hard to know if the problem was that Dad simply wasn't safe at home, or if he hadn't yet found the right companion.

After this traumatic week the agency arranged for a new companion to come and take care of Dad. She was wonderful. She was gentle and compassionate. She also was more skilled in terms of his catheter care and diet. She did a good job, and I finally felt like he would be safe with her. But after a week, she told me that the constant lifting and moving my dad was taking its toll on her back. We appreciated her honesty and her professionalism. She didn't want to have Dad fall. And I didn't want her to injure herself so she would be unable to work.

We thanked her, then went back to the agency in search of a new companion. We had a series of meetings with the supervisor to find a new companion and despite changes in companion staff, the failures continued. By this point we had gone through three companions in six weeks.

The ER staff and urology doctors knew me so well from my frequent visits that we were on a first-name basis. I felt like the character Norm on *Cheers*, walking into the bar and being greeted by the regulars.

With each repeated hospitalization, Dad emerged weaker. Because he was bedridden for extended periods of time, he continued to lose weight, strength, and mobility. He had no appetite for the mushy food he was required to eat. We tried literally spoon-feeding him. He'd eat small amounts just to please us. We were literally losing more of him each passing day.

In our hearts we felt we had to try to have him come home to see if he could manage, before we were forced to move on to the inevitable next step, which was a nursing home. I knew intellectually it was the right decision. It was the only way that Dad would have professional around-the-clock help available to him. I also understood this meant he would never return home. His level of functioning would probably continue to decline unless we could get him to eat and engage in physical and occupational therapies.

I found a nursing home that had a good reputation for the therapies it offered. It was also near where I lived. We transferred my dad there. It was amazing how Dad never complained about any of these decisions. We were lucky. He trusted that the decisions my siblings and I were making for him were the right ones. We always explained to him where he was going and why. We wanted to prepare him for what to expect. During our frequent visits, besides just enjoying his company, we'd keep an eye on him, lend him ongoing support, and observe the staff that was working with him.

At the nursing home, Dad's pattern of eating—taking only a few bites of his pureed food—continued. He only ate more with our urging, but all too quickly he'd say, *"No mas"*: Spanish for "No more." He continued to lose weight in spite of the therapists working with him. By now he'd lost over thirty pounds.

My siblings didn't like this nursing home. Soon after Dad arrived, Danny called. He asked me to rate it on a scale of one to ten, with ten being the best. My frame of reference was based on my experience as a social worker; I'd been to many nursing homes in my work, so I thought about both the best and the worst places I had visited. I told him it was between a six and a seven. Susie rated it as a two, and when on a visit she heard a confused resident begin shouting, she dropped her rating to a one. She felt we should explore additional nursing homes for Dad. She didn't believe he was getting enough therapy and proper care where he was. I encouraged her to check out other options.

Susie discovered a place nearby that had been originally created for German Jews and Holocaust survivors arriving in Chicago in the 1940s. Over the years its program had expanded and now offered all levels of care including hospice. I was amazed that this facility had been here in my hometown for so many years, and we had never heard of it.

Susie and I went for a visit and to meet with the staff. We immediately knew it was the right place for Dad and for us. We were not religious. But I found it interesting that during times of crisis we sometimes fell back on the beliefs we rejected as we were growing up.

We were surprised by how much comfort we took in talking with the administrative staff. They were totally accepting of our concerns and care requests. In addition, a doctor was on staff there. They had a strong group of physical, occupational, and speech therapists.

The facility also had a huge rooftop deck, with all kinds of flowers, and a wonderful view of the Chicago skyline. Dad was so looking forward to getting outside and being in the sunshine.

We would continue to visit and to advocate for him, of course, but in a very real way Dad's future was in their hands. All we could do was to wait. I hated feeling so helpless. I prayed they could produce the miraculous turnaround in his health for which we all were hoping.

It seemed that finally, Dad was in good hands. He was with staff that could be trusted. They were invested in working with him and caring for him. On the day that Dad was admitted there, I slept through the night for the first time in months.

At my request, the staff immediately included me in their meetings. This meant I had daily input on their treatment goals. And I wanted to learn about any medical concerns they had about Dad. I was happy to see that they felt comfortable approaching me with their questions. Our family made it clear to them that we were realistic about

Dad's failing health. We had candid discussions about what measures would be taken or not taken in terms of his care.

Over the years, Dad and I had numerous conversations about what he wanted us to do if he ever became seriously ill. He also had created a living will, which gave me medical power of attorney, allowing me to make decisions about his treatment and care if he was unable to. It was a huge relief for me knowing that the decisions I was relaying to the staff were in unison with his beliefs and wishes. I was so grateful we'd had those discussions. It took away the burden of imagining I might make choices that would not have been his.

Dad quickly settled in. His sense of humor was intact, and he proceeded to immediately charm the staff. He told his doctor playfully, "At the hospital doctors are like confetti—there are way too many of them in one place at one time."

I was glad to see how he'd engaged his caregivers with his humor and easygoing ways. Yet I couldn't keep from assessing Dad as I had done for so many years during my career. Sometimes knowing more puts you at a disadvantage. I saw how little he was eating. The speech therapist was amazing, and she tried so hard to help him. I would sit with her and Dad, watching as she patiently spent over an hour and a half at each meal, coaxing him to eat small bites of food. I was so grateful. But I also knew that this amount of nutrition could not sustain him. The nursing staff, speech therapist, doctor, my siblings, and I all agreed with Dad's decision to not be fed by a tube or be forced to eat.

As the weeks went by, Dad continued to lose weight and grow weaker. He needed oxygen, even when he was simply sitting in his wheelchair. Yet he still smiled and continued to joke with my siblings and me when we visited him. Caryn came from England and Danny from California.

We repeatedly tried to gently coax him to keep eating as much as he could. We also encouraged him to participate in his therapies as much as possible. However, with his nutritional intake steadily decreasing, his memory and ability to think also diminished. He became more confused, especially at night.

One afternoon I came to visit Dad. He was in the patient lounge after eating just a few spoonfuls of pureed food at lunch. He looked tired and very thin. His eyes weren't focused on anything in particular, and it was clearly hard for him to focus on me after I greeted him.

"I've just come back from work and I'm tired," he told me.

"You're ninety-seven now, Dad," I answered gently. "Maybe it's time to retire and just relax for a while. You deserve it."

"No, I need to take care of my family." Then he went on, almost in a whisper: "I had a dream about Susie. She's thin, and she often complains about being cold. I knew she was cold, so I put her under the covers to keep her warm." He also told me about a dream with Danny in it. In the dream, Dad said, he was taking care of Danny.

Dad is quickly moving toward the end of his life, I thought, *yet his focus remains on taking care of his family.*

It was a long, tearful drive home.

I went back to the facility the next day. Just as I stepped out the elevator I saw the physical therapist working with a man who was trying as hard as he could just to stand up. The patient was shaking and frail. He was barely able to rise. I suddenly realized this man was my father. By now he had dropped thirty-four pounds and he was too weak to even stand up without somebody pulling him up.

Dad was trying the best he could. It was heartbreaking to see how limited he had become.

When I came to visit Dad the next day, he was lying in his bed and looked like he was sleeping. I sat next to his bed and gently touched his arm. "No more, Dad," I said quietly. "*No mas*. It's okay for you to let go and rest. We love you and when you're ready to leave us, we're ready to let you go in peace."

Even though he didn't open his eyes or respond, I had no doubt that he heard me. I believed I had to give him permission to die, so that he would understand that if he was ready, we were too. There is an intimacy to this moment that is difficult to explain if you have not lived through it with someone you love. It is powerful, poignant, and incredibly painful. It is also pure and honest communication born from love and mutual respect.

Three hours later, I got a call from his nurse. "I think your father is dying," he told me. "His pulse is very weak and his breathing is slow. You'd better get over here fast."

I rushed out the door and made the ten-minute drive as quickly as I could. I ran from the elevator and there was the nurse. I saw his sad face and immediately knew that Dad had died.

"In the minute I took to call you and went back to your father's room," he explained, "he stopped breathing."

I told the nurse about the conversation I had earlier with my dad. I was now more certain than ever that he had heard my words.

In my work, I had been with many patients as they had died. The transition from life to death can be a very peaceful one, as it was for Dad. He had no pain. His organs shut down. I truly believed he had made the decision to just let go of life.

I walked in his room with tears in my eyes and held his hand and kissed him. Living had become so hard for him. He had passed into that arena where the quality of his life had diminished so much that maybe, just maybe, he would welcome death. Earlier, he had made it clear that he had no fear about death and dying.

It had been so hard to see my formerly vibrant, healthy father struggling so hard to simply live. I loved him so much. Now I needed some time to literally catch my breath. I had to acknowledge to myself that he was truly gone.

It doesn't matter how old you are when you lose a parent. It can be a surprise even when you expect it. You are and always will be his or her child. Your relationship is unique and can never be replaced. It remains a loss no matter what the circumstances.

For the last couple of weeks, I'd kept the number of the funeral home in my purse. As soon as I'd called Susie, Caryn, and Danny, I called the funeral home to let them know my father had died. We needed to make arrangements to have his body picked up. I had put aside a suit, shoes, and socks for his burial when it was time. As I was thinking about all this, it was clear to me how realistic I'd been about Dad's deteriorating health. Still, none of this seemed real to me. How could he be gone?

I realized that from this moment on, the decisions being made would be ours only—my siblings' and mine.

Dad's voice was gone. We would do our best to honor his wishes and be true to the person he was. I had promised him his funeral would reflect his service to his country. He was so proud of that. And it was important to me that his funeral would also highlight his humor, his humanity, and his love for his family and friends. He'd taught us about these things, and more. He was no longer there to help guide us, but he had instilled much of who he was in us.

He was not a pretentious man. No false accolades, no pretense about wealth. He didn't care what other people thought about him. As I sat at his bedside, gazing at this man who was so thin and so pale, I was flooded with wonderful memories from our past.

It was a beautiful day, warm and sunny, as the limousine carrying my siblings and me followed the hearse carrying the body of our father to the cemetery. We saw the army insignia on the side of his hearse. There was no doubt this would have made Dad proud.

When we drove past the uniformed honor guard, saluting, it was impossible to hold back the tears. They stood tall, straight, and strong, moving in cadence together, slowly and respectfully.

We sat by my father's graveside, surrounded by friends and family. The honor guard stood in full salute. The lonely horn played "Taps," which echoed throughout the cemetery. With pinpoint precision the honor guard folded the flag, which had been draped over Dad's coffin. We'd decided to have them present it to Danny, the only son. I was deeply moved, and so glad that we'd been able to fulfill Dad's wishes.

Later, many people came up to me to tell me that Dad's funeral was the most touching one they had ever been to. In turn, we shared a few stories about Dad, wanting to help them know what kind of man he was, and what he meant to his family. That was what we all wanted. That would have been what Dad wanted, although he never would have liked being the center of attention. As he would have said, *no mas.*

PART TWO

Introduction to Part Two

This next section of the book contains resources and information critical for those involved in caretaking for their parents or other elderly loved ones. I wanted to look in more depth at relevant topics that we may not have faced in taking care of my father. These are the primary challenges that I find are commonly shared among those in the caretaking position. This includes topics like how to manage hospital bills and insurance, who takes on what caretaker responsibility, what you need to know about nursing homes, and Medicare versus Medicaid. In addition, this part of the book discusses challenges like estate planning, what happens when the body ages, finding the right nursing home, and coping with death. In the final chapter, there is a compilation of additional resources for those who wish to delve deeper. The chapter headings will help you focus on the information that may be most relevant to your situation. I hope you find it helpful as you face the inevitable challenges that arise when you find yourself in the role of caretaker.

Chapter 9

How to Manage Hospital and Insurance Bills

One of the toughest aspects of managing health care for your elderly loved one is simply keeping track of medical and hospital bills.

What is the first thing you can do to make this process go smoothly? Have him give written permission for you to have access to all his medical records and hospital bills. You'll need to be able to look at these records to properly manage payments. This also gives you the freedom to speak directly to the providers if necessary. And you should get a release of records and information form signed by the senior so that medical staff can speak with you as inevitably, questions do come up.

It's a good idea for you to have a copy of all your senior loved one's medical records. The information in these records—which will include test results—can be extremely useful if he has to see another health care provider. Supplying them with this info can save him from undergoing any additional unnecessary testing. A release of records is usually needed to do this, and there is a fee associated with copying these records.

I recommend that you start by creating a hard-copy file. Also, if possible, create a spreadsheet to keep track of the following information:

- What bills came in?

- What service are the bills for?

- Who is the provider of service?

- What is the date of service?

- What date did you pay the bill?

- How was it paid? For example, check number or which credit card?

- What amount did you pay out-of-pocket?

- What amount did your insurance company pay for each service?

There's a good chance that you'll be receiving piles of paperwork. You'll get a bill from the hospital, doctor, nursing home, radiologist, therapist, or visiting nurse when your parent receives any of these services. In addition to the bill, you'll be sent a letter called an explanation of benefits, or EOB. The EOB is not a bill and it usually says that. Its purpose is to inform the recipient of services as to what part of his medical treatment is covered/eligible under his insurance plan. All EOBs include the following information:

- Date of service

- The name of the provider

- The patient name and the type of treatment/service that was provided

- The fee charged by the provider

- The amount the insurance company paid the provider

- The amount of money that's owed to the provider

- Amount taken off the bill for a preferred provider

These letters are generated when the health-care professional or agency from whom your parent is receiving services sends a bill to your insurance administrator. If your parent's provider is in your insurance network, a provider discount is included in your coverage. As noted above, this will show up on your EOB and your insurance bills.

Your senior's insurance coverage is usually better when she works with health-care agencies or providers that are in her network. Depending on her financial situation, this may need to be considered when she is getting medical treatment. If you call the number on her insurance card, you can get information regarding the agencies and providers that are in her network. You can usually find this information on her insurance company's website by inputting information such as the name or specialty of the provider and where it/they are located. They are often referred to as "preferred providers." They often participate in PPO plans. (More about PPOs on page 223.)

Health maintenance organizations, or HMOs, also have specific providers associated with their network of medical treatment. You can find out more by calling the number on your senior's insurance card and/or accessing the HMO's website. (There's also more information on HMOs on page 222.)

Keep in mind that it can take weeks or months for insurance companies to process the insurance claims they receive. Do *not* pay your senior's health-care provider's bill until you've reviewed the corresponding EOB, outlining the amount she is responsible for paying. Sometimes providers will send out a bill before the claim is processed by the insurance carrier.

Keep the EOB attached to the corresponding bill you paid. File them by date of service or by provider name, or whatever system works for you. I suggest keeping them all together in one place so that you have easy access to it.

Above, I mentioned creating paper files. I found these very useful when I was helping to take care of my parents. Get file folders and label each folder with a provider name, such as the hospital, doctor, or therapist. Then as you receive the bills and EOBs, you can place them in the corresponding folder, along with notes on what you did, such as when you paid a bill and by what means.

When you contact health-care providers regarding billing or with other questions on behalf of your loved one, always make a notation of these items:

- The question(s) you asked

- The response(s) you got

- The name of the person(s) with whom you spoke

- The date and time you spoke with him/her

- Who he/she is—e.g., a customer-service representative in the billing office, a manager, etc.

Keep the notes from these conversations with the associated bill and EOB in case you need to review them or make a follow-up call. You may need to reference this information if the person does not follow up as promised.

You might be amazed to learn how often there are errors in billing associated with health-care services. Sometimes a doctor may use a wrong code that can cause a denial of coverage. Patients who are hospitalized can accidentally be charged for services they never received or be charged twice. There are numerous reasons why a claim may be denied.

Hospital bills can be especially overwhelming because they have a multitude of services and providers associated with them. You may see names you're not familiar with: for example, an anesthesiologist who provided anesthesia for your parent's surgery.

Be sure that you know all the providers who are billing for their services—and that those services you're seeing on the bill/EOB are correct. Delehanty and Ginzler in *Caring for Your Parents* advise to look for errors such as these:

- Incorrect name, address, or Social Security number

- Incorrect dates of service (which usually should not include the day your parent is discharged)

- Wrong or duplicate orders for room fees, medication, tests, or supplies

- Excessive operating room time

They go on to recommend that you "Don't put off dealing with hospital bills, no matter how overworked you are or how bizarre they seem. Within ninety days, most hospitals will turn over late bills to collection agencies."

What do you do if you think that a claim is not being fairly handled? If you believe that an insurer is unfairly denying a claim, contact its member services department and ask how to appeal a claim. State and Federal laws protect your parent's right to proper health insurance practices. If the insurer is uncooperative, you may file a written complaint with your state insurance regulation bureau.

If your senior is unable to pay his health-care bill, talk to a representative in the provider's business office. See if you can negotiate a payment plan. Sometimes, if your senior has limited funds, you may even be able to have his bill reduced. Hospitals and health-care providers would rather get some money than no money. If your senior is contacted by collection agencies and receiving threats, step in. Go directly back to the provider to see what kind of an agreement can be made. Make sure you get this agreement in writing. Write everything down, including the name of the person you spoke with, so you'll have this information for future reference if disputes occur.

Don't be afraid to contact the billing office at a hospital or the billing staff of your senior's other providers. You may need to get clarification on a bill or to question a claim or charge that doesn't appear to be correct. It can feel intimidating to make these calls, but it's important to follow up if you believe an error has occurred.

When you call, have your senior's bill, the claim, and any notes you have about this health-care service right in front of you. Be ready to provide the claim or account number.

As I discussed above, there will be an interval between when your senior receives a service and when she is billed for it. Today many health-care providers have an efficient business component to their offices, and bills may arrive very quickly.

Make sure that when your loved one receives a bill, you're able to review it promptly and address it in a reasonably prompt fashion as best you can. This will help avoid the involvement of a collection agency.

The process of sorting through medical bills and claims can feel daunting. Recently I helped a family member with her paperwork. When we sat down together, I found that she had over 150 pages of medical bills and EOBs. She was very anxious and overwhelmed as she showed me all the pages.

We started by dividing the paperwork into piles based on provider and then we matched each bill with the corresponding EOB. We then placed them in order by the date of service and created file folders based on the piles we'd created. Now when she gets a new bill or EOB, she simply pulls out the matching folder and she has an up-to-date record on what was paid or what needs to be paid for each provider. It's a very useful system.

I talked earlier about creating a spreadsheet. If you're good with computers, it can be a great tool. But again, it's still a good idea to keep the paperwork. Bills, EOBs, and so on can arrive a year or more after a person has gotten treatment. These records must be available as a reference point.

It can sometimes be tempting to just toss this mail aside when you're looking through it, especially if you're dealing with the ongoing care needs of an ill loved one or, even worse, dealing with the loss of that loved one. It can be difficult to focus. Nonetheless, try to tackle the paperwork as soon as possible. Taking action will help the task feel a bit more manageable.

Deciphering the Language of Insurance

The term "deductible" is frequently used in association with health insurance. A deductible is a specific amount of money you must pay for your health care before your insurance company begins to offer you benefits coverage. Your deductible is determined on an annual basis. This means you have to pay your deductible every year before your benefits are initiated. If and when you do meet your deductible, you still must continue to pay for things like your insurance premiums. Some plans have individual deductibles and some have family deductibles. If you're helping your parent decide which type of deductible is most beneficial, consider his past patterns of utilizing health care.

Generally speaking, when you select a plan with a higher deductible, your insurance premiums—which are paid monthly or every couple of months—will be lower. The money you pay toward your deductible goes toward your out-of-pocket expenses.

Be sure you know what your senior's out-of-pocket maximum is with his insurance company coverage. "Out of pocket" refers to the expenses that he must pay; they're not paid by his health insurance company. Examples of out-of-pocket expenses would be copayments and deductibles. Once he reaches his maximum out-of-pocket coverage, his insurance company usually will begin picking up 100 percent of the costs per his individual insurance plan.

Another common term used in relation to health insurance is "copayment" or "copay." A copay is a specific amount of money you must pay immediately when you get certain health-care services. For example, when you see a physician you might have to pay $20 or $30 up-front, regardless of the cost of or the reason for your visit. Often you can find the amount of your copay noted on the back of your insurance card.

There are basically two types of health insurance plans that your parent can choose from, although they can be packaged in many different ways. The two major plan categories are managed health plans, like HMOs, and fee-for-service health insurance, like Blue Cross Blue Shield.

Health maintenance organizations, or HMOs, have a provider network that a person is required to use. You cannot see any practitioner out of this network without incurring costs that you must pay out-of-pocket. You generally must select a primary care physician (PCP), who is the person you will see most often. If your medical condition requires a specialist, this doctor will refer you to the appropriate health-care practitioner in this provider network.

Your PCP will be the one to continue to manage or coordinate your care with any other necessary practitioners. Generally speaking, an HMO plan may offer your parent lower deductibles and copays, but there are more restrictions on what you can do.

Fee-for-service health-care plans offer you the freedom to select your own physician. If you need to see a specialist, it's generally not required that you get a referral from your primary care physician. It also gives you more latitude in terms of which hospital you go to. This type of program will generally have out-of-pocket maximums. The deductibles for this type of plan are usually higher than those of HMOs.

Preferred provider organizations, or PPOs, are a popular choice for many. They're similar to HMOs in the sense that you must choose a provider from a designated network in order to get the maximum coverage from your insurance company. If you go out of this network, you'll have to pay more. One significant difference is that you're not required to use your primary care physician as a referral source to see another provider.

There is an additional model that is frequently used. It's called a point-of-service plan, or POS. In this type of plan, you have more freedom and control. You can decide to select either a PPO or HMO type of system. The choice you make will determine how much your copay and deductible will be.

Another term you should know is "coinsurance." Coinsurance refers to your portion of the cost that's due for a particular type of health-care service. Your costs begin when you have met your deductible. The specific costs vary depending on the parameters of your plan. For example, once you've met your deductible, if your insurance pays 80 percent, then you would be responsible for 20 percent of the fees. That would be your coinsurance. Be aware that the lower your monthly payments are, the higher your coinsurance will probably be.

Some people find it useful to use an insurance agent (also called "insurance broker"). When your job does not offer a specific set of health insurance options, this may be an alternative for you. These agents work with people of all ages regardless of employment status. Their role is to find insurance based on the client's health and financial parameters. They try to create new business for insurance companies. Sometimes they work for a particular insurance company. These are exclusive agents and can be on salary with the insurance carrier.

Other agents may have multiple insurance companies as clients. They are independent contractors. They also sell different types of insurance including life, health, and disability insurance. They can help you get the best coverage at the best price.

The benefit of using an insurance agent is they can help you examine your health-care needs and your past use of these types of services. These agents can explain the pros and cons of a particular insurance plan in terms of your specific coverage needs. In addition, insurance brokers also answer any questions you have regarding your plan before and after you have purchased it.

Insurance agents are independent contractors for the insurance agencies that they represent. These agents are either on salary with a specific insurance agency or get a commission when they sell a policy. You do not have to pay them for their services.

What Is the Impact of the Affordable Care Act?

The Affordable Care Act (ACA) legislation has made sig nificant changes in health care that directly impact many people. This legislation was designed to help consumers have additional control over their health care. Some of the highlights include:

- Lifetime limits on many benefits are not permitted anymore.

- Insurance companies are now required to publicly demonstrate reasons for large increases in insurance rates.

- Anyone under the age of nineteen cannot be denied health-care coverage for a preexisting condition.

- Preventive care such as immunizations and blood-pressure screenings are paid for.

- You choose your primary care doctor from your health-care network.

- You can get emergency treatment at a hospital outside of your network.

- You have the right to appeal to your carrier when a denial of coverage occurs.

The most important thing anyone can do when helping an aging loved one with health insurance is be thoughtful about choosing the plan that will be most useful for them. Be sure you understand how much your senior will have to pay for his health care out of their pocket before the insurance coverage begins. Think about what is a priority for him. Would he rather be the one to pick his doctor or hospital? Is it better for him financially to pay a lower deductible and have a higher out-of-pocket maximum if he is in good health? How often does he need to see a specialist, use medication, or go to the hospital? Is it better to get coverage on an individual basis or as a family?

Don't be afraid to ask questions as together you look through material outlining the health-care insurance options available to him. If there is a human resources person where you work, she or he can be an excellent resource as you and your senior weigh this important decision.

Chapter 10

Preventing Identity Theft

The news is filled with reports about stolen credit-card numbers. Incidents of identity theft seem to be growing in scope and frequency. Seniors are a tempting target for these types of crimes. Elderly people tend to be more trusting, and that makes them more vulnerable.

A recent example occurred when the Affordable Care Act (ACA) was being initiated. Scam artists would contact seniors and persuade them to reveal their Social Security numbers and other private information. The scammers would say they were working with the government, and that they needed this information in order for the seniors to receive benefits from the ACA.

The elderly are also targeted because thieves assume they have more money than do young people. In addition, they tend to have a more isolated lifestyle. They don't always use computers to keep close track of their credit-card accounts.

Going online to check bills is not something many seniors are familiar with. And they may not pay as much attention to the paper bills they receive due to visual, memory, or organizational problems. The elderly tend to be at home more often, and thus are around when scam calls are made or when people knock on their door with illegal schemes.

When seniors do leave their homes, they also can be more vulnerable to thieves, especially if they have assistive devices such as walkers, canes, or wheelchairs. Diminished hearing and vision can limit their awareness of people around them. They may be less alert when a pickpocket snatches a wallet. A senior at an ATM machine may also be more at risk for a thief looking to rob someone.

So what can your elderly loved one do? And if you're helping her with her mail and/or paying bills, what can you do to safeguard her identity? Here are some suggestions.

- She shouldn't carry extra identification, financial records, or credit cards with her. She generally doesn't need to have a Medicare card with her unless she's getting a prescription filled or receiving medical treatment.

- Invest in a paper shredder. Any documents with names, addresses, driver's license number, Social Security number, bank statements, deposit slips, credit-card account information, and financial records should be shredded. Never leave receipts in an open area.

- Discourage your senior from giving money to people who solicit on the phone no matter who they say they are affiliated with. She shouldn't stay on the phone and let them engage her in more conversation as a way of persuading her to give them money. If she wants to give this organization money, get a phone number from a legitimate source and contact them directly.

- If she uses a computer regularly, make sure it has the proper software to protect against viruses and from people who try to steal information. Password information should be stored in a secure place. She should use different passwords for various accounts, and they should be changed regularly.

- Her credit reports should be regularly checked in order to ensure that no unauthorized activity has occurred. This should be done only by legitimate companies. The three major credit card bureaus are Equifax at 800-525-6285, Transunion at 800-680-7289, and Experian at 888-397-3742. If your senior becomes a victim of fraud, help her contact her credit-card bureau so that they can be on the alert. She should also contact her credit-card company, or companies, immediately.

- She should have a safety-deposit box in a bank. If she is homebound, consider getting a safe in which to store her confidential documents, jewelry, cash, checkbooks, passports, and other important personal records and/or small valuables.

- If she's using checks to pay her bills, make sure she doesn't put her entire Social Security number on the check. She should just use the last four digits. That's enough proof of identity.

- When she goes on vacation, make sure she's put a stop on her mail, or that a reliable person is available to pick it up while she's out of town.

- Does she go to ATM machines? Encourage her to be aware of the people around her. She can use her body or her hand to shield the information she's inputting into the ATM's computer. This prevents those who might be watching from getting PIN numbers or other personal log-in information.

- Make sure she reports attempted fraud episodes involving her Social Security number to Medicare via the Social Security Administration. Also, help her contact her local law-enforcement representatives. This act can help prevent future crimes.

- Talk with her about not being fooled by claims of "free" products or programs. This can be a ploy to lure people into giving money down the line.

- If she's being approached by someone who is making some type of sales pitch, and she's intent on pursuing it, ensure that you participate in her discussions with the salesperson. Do some research to find out if it's a legitimate offer.

Unfortunately, there are all kinds of scams that unscrupulous people use in order to trick vulnerable seniors into revealing information that can assist them in accessing valuable personal data. According to the usa.gov website, here are some of the most common schemes:

Telemarketing

An ID thief may call and make fraudulent offers for products, benefits, or other medical services. The caller will require you to provide personal information such as your Social Security number, birthday, or Medicare ID number.

Tax ID Theft

Phony tax preparers steal your Social Security number and sell it to scammers. ID thieves may also read obituaries so they can file a tax return in the deceased person's name. This can be a problem for a surviving spouse, when he or she tries to file taxes later in the tax season. For more information contact the IRS's Taxpayer Advocate Service at 877-275-8271.

Medical ID Theft

In general, seniors have more contact with medical service providers that can take advantage of access to their insurance information to get medical services in their name, or to issue fraudulent billing to them and their health insurer.

Nursing Home and Long-Term Care

Staff at these facilities have access to a senior's personal information on file, as well as the potential misuse or theft of a senior's finances (checkbooks or financial statements in the senior's room). You can report this fraud to the long-term care ombudsman in your state. Type in long-term-care ombudsman and your state to find your local state organization.

If your senior has visiting nurses or therapists, or home caregivers, he should never leave any important records in places where they are easily accessed or visible. Be certain that none of the information described above is discarded in a garbage can and thrown out. This can be a treasure trove for people interested in stealing a person's identity. Any documents or mail with identifying information should be shredded or ripped up before it goes in his garbage can or recycling bin outside.

Seniors in assisted-living facilities or nursing homes also have people coming in and out of their apartments or rooms regularly. This may include nursing staff, cleaning staff, repairmen, maintenance staff, therapists, or other family members or friends of roommates. Don't leave personal information on top of dressers or desks. There may not be any truly secure places to keep things in a nursing home, so you may want to make sure these identifying documents are safely stored or locked up in your possession, or in that of a trusted relative or friend.

Want to learn more about handling identity theft and fraud? Here are some additional resources:

- The Federal Trade Commission Bureau of Consumer Protection. Phone number: 202-326-2222. Fraud hotline: 877-382-4357. Website: www.consumer.ftc.gov.

- National Fraud Information Center helps victims of fraud that's committed over the Internet or on the phone. Phone number: 800-876-7060. Website: www.fraud.org.

- American Association of Retired Persons (AARP) offers advice on how to avoid credit scams, fraud, and identity theft. Phone number: 888-687-2277. Website: www.aarp.org/money/scams-fraud/.

- Fraud Hotline for Seniors via the Senate Special Committee on Aging. Phone number: 855-303-9470. Website: www.aging.senate.gov/fraud-hotline.

- The National Center for Victims of Crime is a resource and advocacy program offering help and support to people of all ages who are victims of crimes. They offer referrals for attorneys who have expertise in helping crime victims. Address: 2000 M Street, NW, Suite 480, Washington, DC, 20036. Phone number: 202-467-8700. Website (which has lots of resource information): www.victimsofcrime.org/.

- National Association of Bunco Investigators (NABI) is a nonprofit organization whose primary goal is to identify and catch con artists and criminals involved in all kinds of scams and illegal schemes. Website: www.nabihq.org.

- The National Criminal Justice Reference Service offers special publications that address issues relating to elder fraud and financial abuse. Website: www.ncjrs.gov.

Identity theft can happen to anyone. While I was writing this chapter I went to my bank to get a new credit card. The banker told me that someone was in their national database under my Social Security number. I was shocked. I thought I'd done everything right. I had been very careful not to put much online regarding my financial information. All my credit-card bills and statements were carefully reviewed. All my receipts were shredded. I carefully discarded mail making sure my name and address were removed. When I used my credit card I was aware of anyone being close by who could possibly see the numbers.

The banker told me she understood how I felt because she had been a victim as well. She advised me to contact the Social Security Administration and the credit-card bureaus (they're listed on page 229) to send out a fraud alert. I did that as soon as I got home.

I later learned that someone had incorrectly put in my Social Security number in some sort of national database to which banks have access when people are applying for credit. After doing research on my behalf, my banker realized it was an error and noted it.

Even though I was lucky and no actual fraud had been committed, I really learned my lesson. A couple of days later I got an "automated" phone call allegedly from my bank, telling me that my credit card had been deactivated. The automated call said I needed to punch in my credit-card number on the telephone keys. I hung up and immediately called my credit-card company. The representative confirmed that they never make any type of call like that.

We all need to be careful about protecting our personal

information in order to prevent potential identity theft. Especially if you're helping take care of an elderly loved one, being cautious can save you both lots of time, money, and months or even years of aggravation as you try to correct the damage caused by the perpetrators of these crimes.

Chapter 11

What You Need to Know about Nursing Homes

Sometimes making the choice to move your senior loved one to a nursing home feels right and there's no anxiety about the decision. However, for many seniors and their families, making this choice can be difficult and scary. Often, they are uncertain as to what it will be like to live there, and how the transition will go. It's a big adjustment.

Nursing homes are an option for people who need ongoing supervision for health and safety reasons. They may need daily assistance with their personal-care needs, such as bathing, dressing, and eating. These facilities also provide round-the-clock nursing care for those who need help with medication management (including intravenous medication), or nutrition, oxygen, or catheter care.

They also cater to people needing special attention in managing skin care to prevent breakdown. When breakdown occurs, it can lead to other health-care complications such as infection. When left untreated, this type of infection can possibly result in death.

For people who have ongoing medical problems, being in a nursing home and having this additional professional help can be vitally important.

Key Tips When Searching for a Nursing Home

When you're thinking about a nursing home, try to find a place that's geographically close to the family members or friends who will be visiting the most frequently. If the facility staff knows that your loved one will have regular contact with family members or friends, it can help ensure that a higher level of care is consistently being offered to her. It shouldn't be this way, but I have seen it over and over again.

Make sure you meet and get the names and contact info of the key staff members who will be providing care to your loved one. This may include nurses, doctors, and aides, as well as recreational, physical, occupational, and speech therapists. Questions may arise where you'll need to speak directly with an individual practitioner regarding specific issues relating to your loved one.

Make it a point to meet the director of the facility to get insights about his or her philosophy regarding patient treatment; make sure it is congruent with your beliefs. The social worker and/or staff in the billing office can also be very helpful in terms of explaining your senior's Medicare, Medicaid, and insurance coverage and what out-of-pocket costs you'll need to anticipate.

What Type of Nursing Care Does Your Senior Need?

Nursing homes can offer a variety of levels of care. For example, some programs offer special units for residents who have different types of dementia, which causes problems with memory and can create episodes of confusion. There is greater staff supervision and patient support on these wings or floors. Other wings/floors offer skilled care for residents who need ongoing assistance with their mobility and self-care needs. Residents who are dealing with complex medical diagnoses receive a higher level of nursing care.

What about the Cost?

The other factor you must consider is the cost of the nursing facility and what financial resources are available to your elderly loved one.

The cost of nursing homes can vary. Many people must use their savings and assets to cover the long-term costs of nursing-home care. Some nursing homes have beds that are slated for Medicaid residents. (Medicaid is funded through the state.) These beds can be an option for people with limited financial resources who meet the state income-eligibility requirements.

Here are some important aspects related to nursing-home care and Medicaid coverage that can be found on the medicaid.gov site:

- You may have to pay out-of-pocket for nursing-home care each month. The nursing home will bill Medicaid for the rest of the amount. How much you owe depends on your income and deductions.

- The state can't put a lien on your home if there is a reasonable chance you will return home after getting nursing-home care or if you have a spouse or dependents living there.

- Most people who are eligible for Medicaid must reduce their assets first. There are rules about what is counted as an asset and what isn't when determining Medicaid eligibility. There are also rules that require states to allow married couples to protect a certain amount of assets and income when one of them is in an institution like a nursing home.

- Transferring your assets for less than fair market value may subject you to a penalty

that Medicaid won't pay for your nursing-
home care for a period of time. How long
that period is depends on the value of the
assets you give away. There are limited
exceptions to this, especially if you have
a spouse, or a blind or disabled child.
Generally, giving away your assets can result
in no payment for your nursing-home care,
sometimes for months or even years.

• To apply for medical assistance, call your
  state Medicaid office. They can tell you if
  you qualify for the Medicaid nursing-home
  benefit or other programs.

Some people want to be proactive and purchase long-
term health insurance. This helps financially prepare for a time
in the future where they may need to enter a long-term care
program like those offered by nursing homes. These types of
insurance policies are becoming more commonly advertised.
The coverage varies a great deal. The costs are always lower
if a person starts when she is younger and in good health. A
monthly premium is paid for this type of coverage.

If your senior has purchased this type of plan, hopefully
she'll have investigated the carrier to be certain it's a legitimate
program and has the proper licensing. Make sure that both
you and your senior understand what the coverage is. What
types of care and facilities are eligible for coverage? The last
thing you want is to be unpleasantly surprised by your senior
having no coverage at a time when she needs it the most.

Medicare does not cover long-term room and board costs. If a resident has specific skilled-care needs, such as intravenous medication, or daily physical, occupational, or speech therapy, there may be some short-term coverage from Medicare. This depends on the patient's diagnosis and doctor-recommended care plan. Medicare will not cover the cost of a companion, aide, or registered nurse who stays bedside with a resident in a nursing home to ensure she doesn't fall, engage in unsafe behavior, or have specific, ongoing, frequent-care needs.

Finding the Right Nursing Home

There are a variety of ways to learn about which nursing home is the right one for your elderly loved one. Do visit the facilities you're considering in order to see firsthand what they're like. If your loved one is able to visit, it can be a good idea to take him as well once you've narrowed the possibilities down. This gives him an opportunity to see for himself what the facility is like. He can also personally meet and interact with the staff.

For many people, one of the most difficult aspects of moving to a nursing home is the feeling that they've lost control over how and when they do things. It's also very challenging to become dependent on others for care and mobility. There can be a real sense of loss. Some people worry about their safety and feel vulnerable not only in terms of the staff but sometimes other patients. They may be concerned about a loss of privacy, especially in situations where they must share their rooms with a roommate.

As you walk through a nursing home, observe the interactions between staff and residents. Does the staff treat their patients with dignity and respect? Is staff courteous to each other?

In *The Eldercare Handbook*, Stella Mora Henry offers these additional tips:

Greetings

Are you greeted as you enter the facility? There are reasons why this is significant. First, this is the resident's home; we all greet company as they enter our home to indicate they are welcome. Second, it is important for staff to know who is entering the building.

Acknowledgment and Morale

As you walk down the halls, do the staff members smile and acknowledge you? Do you have a sense of staff morale? High morale is a benchmark of quality care.

Odor

Does the odor of urine permeate the building? Keep in mind that if a nurse has just finished changing a resident and has carried soiled clothing to the designated bin in the hallway, there will be a temporary odor that should dissipate in five to ten minutes. But if the odor is persistent, poor housekeeping or inadequate nursing may be responsible.

Grooming

Are residents up and dressed appropriately for the time of day and season? Is their hair combed? Are the men shaved and groomed? Are they wearing shoes and socks?

Kindness

Does the staff interact kindly with the residents, addressing them by name, or do they converse as if the residents were not present? Do they speak in demeaning baby talk?

Homelike Atmosphere

Nursing homes are federally regulated to "look like a hospital" with hospital beds, cubicle curtains, and nursing stations. Facilities do, however, have control over atmosphere. Does the nursing home have a homelike feel? In residents' rooms, are there family pictures on the walls and nightstands? Are there afghans or comforters on the beds? Are families allowed to bring in favorite chairs or dressers? Is there a pleasant, central gathering area?

Call Bells

When residents ring for help, the call panel at the nurses' station lights up and sounds an alarm to signal the room number. If the alarm persists, the staff is not responding in a timely manner. Ask the person giving the tour how long it should be before a nurse's aide attends to the resident. An acceptable answer is less than five minutes.

Pace

Does the staff appear rushed and tense, as if they have too much to do?

Privacy

If you are touring the facility in the morning—a bathing and dressing period—are residents given privacy? For example, the cubicle curtain should be drawn around the resident's bed during morning care.

Based on my professional experience visiting nursing homes, there are additional criteria for quality care that you should be aware of.

It's a good idea to visit a nursing home when meals are being served. Watch how the staff attends to residents who need help eating their food. Pay attention to how many residents are in the dining room instead of their room. Mealtime can be an important social occasion and provide a good opportunity for staff to interact with the residents. How does the food look and smell? How does staff handle a resident who has not eaten?

One of the things I always notice is if there is a schedule showing resident activities. Take a look at the types of

228 • Role Reversal

activity options offered to residents. Is it something your loved one would be able to participate in? Does it cover a wide variety of interests and mental and physical abilities? Are residents encouraged to participate? Is there a recreational therapist on staff coordinating the program? Is there a designated space for recreational activities?

During my career I visited many nursing homes to help ensure that the recommendations I gave my patients and their families were based on my firsthand observations. I always advised them to visit the floor their loved one would be placed on. This would give them a more accurate perception of the unit's atmosphere. Nursing-home floors with patients needing a higher level of care can have a different feel than those with more independent residents.

I also suggested that they ask about the ratio of nurses and aides to patients on all shifts. You may find that some nursing homes have fewer nurses and aides responsible for more residents.

If your senior loved one is going to need some type of physical, occupational, or speech therapy, make sure the facility you're considering has these services available. Are these therapists part of the regular staff or are they brought in on a contracted basis with less frequency? Is there a physician on staff? What about a social worker? The amount and quality of therapy that patients receive can significantly assist in the recovery process.

Something you should know about is The Joint Commission, formerly the Joint Commission on the Accreditation of Healthcare Organizations. This national and highly respected organization sends independent, trained health-care experts to do extensive site visits in and assessments of hospitals, nursing homes, doctors' offices, office-based surgical centers, home-care programs, and mental-health programs. Every aspect of care and the physical plant of a program/facility are carefully reviewed during these visits. If a program/facility receives accreditation from the Joint Commission, it means that it offers a level of treatment and care that meets national standards. Be sure to ask about accreditation when you visit potential nursing homes.

Getting More Details about Specific Facility Policies

For many people it helps to have their personal possessions with them as they transition to a nursing facility. It can feel more like home and less like an institutional setting. Find out what the rules are about bringing furniture, TVs, or other possessions. Will your senior have a room of her own, or a roommate? Don't bring valuable items into rooms that cannot be locked.

Different facilities have different policies. For example, what are the rules about pets, visitors, smoking, and residents having their own telephones? How do the answers match up with the expectations of your senior loved one?

There are also a number of approaches that are used with residents who become agitated or present disruptive behavior challenges. How are these issues handled? Are restraints used? Is it managed by medication? Is the staff encouraged to try different behavior-modification techniques? Is the same staff assigned to the same patients for continuity purposes? If not, how is it determined which staff member works with a specific patient?

These are important questions; their answers will give you important insights about their patient-management techniques. The law mandates that residents be given a policy statement outlining their rights and services; they must understand and sign it. As you narrow your search, I encourage you to read these policy statements.

When you're visiting a facility, pay attention to how many of the residents are out of their rooms in common areas. How many are participating in activities? Are they being encouraged to interact with other residents? There should be some type of schedule visible, offering different types of events and activities for the residents. This is a key quality-of-care indicator.

When you begin the process of exploring different facilities, it may be that you have a network of friends and family who might be a rich resource. Spread the word that you're interested in getting people's input on good and bad experiences at various facilities.

Another helpful resource can be your local senior-citizen center; the staff may be able to provide advice, information, and support. If your loved one is being seen via a visiting-nurse program, they usually have a social worker on staff who can assist you with your research into nursing-home options.

If your parent is moving from a hospital setting into

a nursing home, find out if there's a hospital-based social worker to assist you with discharge planning. I spent a lot of time doing this with my patients and their family members.

You may want to check out a useful site called the National Consumer Voice for Quality Long-term Care. It offers information about local citizen advocates, or ombudsmen. These ombudsmen are familiar with local programs—both in terms of high-quality care and situations where complaints have been filed. Go to http://theconsumervoice.org/ and click on your state; you'll then see the names of local advocates and how to contact them.

Assessing Safety and Compatibility

Patient safety should be a primary goal in any quality nursing-home program. If your senior has memory problems, ask about the facility's safeguards. Is there security at the doors? Specifically, is there a staff person near an exit monitoring resident activity? Are there alarm systems at exits? As you walk around the facility, are you noticing things like carts or other items in hallways that may be limiting residents' mobility? Are there pull cords or emergency help buttons in bedrooms and bathrooms so that a patient can call for help if needed? Things like ripped carpeting or wheelchairs with broken brakes are red flags for potential falls. If you see these types of issues during your tour, you may want to consider another program option.

If your elderly loved one has a roommate, what is the

facility's policy about matching people in the same room together? For example, if your loved one is alert and highly functional, would he be placed in a room with a person who is confused or shouts out frequently? How is it handled if there appears to be a roommate problem? Would they be willing to consider transferring your loved one to another room? What criteria is used to determine this?

It may seem challenging, tedious, or even overwhelming, but I can't stress strongly enough how important this initial legwork and scouting can be. Also, keep in mind that it can be counterproductive to drag your parent to a bunch of different facilities. For one thing, it could be very discouraging for her to see lower-quality programs. This could make her transition very difficult. Go on some tours without her, narrow your choices to one or two facilities, and then, if possible, allow her to go on a tour and participate in making a final selection.

Timing

After your loved one goes into a nursing home, schedule a meeting with the staff within three months or sooner. The purpose of this meeting is to get a sense of how things are going. It's also the time to identify any potential problem areas that need to be addressed quickly. The staff should not have a problem with this. You do need to allow time after your loved one enters a nursing home to give him an opportunity to get accustomed to his roommate (if he has one), the staff, and the various activities and programs. He needs to get used to the day-to-day environment.

Again, keep in mind that this is a huge transition for your parent. Now other people make the rules about scheduling and many other aspects of the daily activities and care. Offer sincere, ongoing support and reassurance that you'll continue to be a part of his life. If visiting is hard because of geographical distance or pressing responsibilities, then try calling and writing. If possible, take your senior out for meals or excursions with family and/or friends. Also, take this time to get to know the staff. As I mentioned earlier, it's good to have them get to know you. If you're involved on an ongoing basis, they will be more apt to alert you to your loved one's progress and any problems that arise.

One more thing to keep in mind: this transition will be an adjustment for you as well. Give yourself time to learn the policies, routines, and staff. Allowing your loved one to be dependent on care from people you don't know can be hard for you, too. It's a learning process for staff as they get to know and understand the personality and needs of a new resident. Patience from all parties and open communication will help this transition proceed more smoothly for all concerned.

Chapter 12

An Overview of Estate Planning

Initiating a discussion about estate planning can be very difficult. Many of us don't want to think about our loved ones becoming sick or dying. It can feel overwhelming to even talk about. Also, an estate plan can be hard to organize and may be costly. These are just some of the reasons why many people choose not to even bring the subject up with their aging parents.

According to *Forbes* magazine, more than 120 million Americans lack updated estate plans or even long-term financial plans. Seniors, says the report, "are putting their assets and health at risk."

Documents such as a living will and other advanced directives are helpful in enhancing communication with the elderly regarding their future health care. (See pages 111–114 in Chapter 4 for additional details about this.)

However, regarding their financial and personal affairs, thoughtful estate planning is a must.

I am not an attorney, and I also want to emphasize that each person's situation is unique. I consulted Fred Weber, JD, a lawyer specializing in estate planning, to help prepare this chapter. My goal for this chapter is to provide a succinct overview of some of the most common aspects of estate planning. I believe it's important to devote a chapter to this topic because disposition of estates can cause hurt feelings among heirs and, worse, it can really tear families apart. In addition, if estate planning is not done properly, the adult children can end up having to pay their parents' estate taxes. This can be a huge burden. I know a family that had a $5 million tax bill after their parent died because she hadn't done any estate planning.

It's incredibly important to take steps regarding estate-planning options while your senior is able to understand legal concepts and what his assets are. He must be able to clearly communicate his wishes concerning his heirs and inheritance. Ideally, it's a team effort that includes your parent/parents and an attorney who specializes in estate planning. It may also involve family members identified by the seniors who can help gather documents, share information, and facilitate candid discussions.

Keep in mind that this is a process, and will probably involve more than one meeting or discussion. Relationships and finances can change. It's not uncommon for seniors to change their minds about whom they wish to bequeath their assets to. In that case, the estate plan may need to be revisited.

You should also know that the laws of estate planning vary from state to state. In addition, our legislators amend the tax laws regularly, so it's critically important to seek out expert advice in these areas.

Seniors need to identify the people they want to carry out their wishes if they are unable to do so. This means determining the following roles:

Guardian

This person would need to be appointed if your loved one becomes unable to manage her financial affairs.

Trustee

A person or persons who are responsible for controlling or administering the contents of a trust as directed by the person who creates the trust agreement.

Beneficiary

A person who is designated in a will, trust, or life insurance policy to receive specified assets or property as stated in the legal document.

Power of Attorney

A designated person to act on your parent's behalf in regard to all financial or legal issues.

Successor Trustee

When a trust is created, this person (or persons) takes responsibility for managing the trust when the grantor dies or is incapacitated. This role is much like that of an executor, with the exception that the successor trustee only controls assets that are in the trust—nothing that's in other parts of the estate. This person is only allowed to do what the trust instructs. He or she can distribute assets in the trust to the designated trust beneficiaries without having to wait to go through probate.

The dissemination of assets *can* be a smooth experience for all concerned. But, again, thoughtful planning is essential. Many lawyers suggest that age sixty-five is a good time to start thinking about an estate plan. One reason for this is that people often retire around this age. It's also the time when people can be required to make decisions regarding distributions from pensions, 401Ks, or IRAs.

The first step in the estate-planning process is to gather all documentation regarding assets, so that current, comprehensive information is available. This is invaluable in making decisions about the distribution of the assets. These documents should be gathered:

- Bank statements

- Insurance policies

- Military records

- Mortgage records

- Records about pensions, IRAs, and 401Ks

- Records about appraisals of jewelry and other personal items

- Records about worth of stocks, bonds, land, and any other assets

- Information about any debts or loans

In considering your elderly loved one's estate planning, certain life events may occur which should trigger a review of a will or estate plan. They include:

- Marriage or divorce

- Addition of new family members through birth or adoption

- Death of a person identified in the will

- Children identified in will who become adults

- Large increase or decrease in senior's assets and the size of her estate

- They include a decision by your senior that she wants to bequeath her assets to someone else, invest in a business, or give to an organization or charity

You should stay in touch with the attorney who helped your loved one draft the documents. At least every few years, ask about current changes in tax laws and if/how they affect your loved one's estate plan. If your parent or your attorney moves to a different area, get a reliable referral for a new attorney with whom to follow up.

The Four Major Documents

Here are the four major documents your senior will need in putting together his estate plan:

1. Last will and testament
2. Health-care proxy
3. Living will or advanced healthcare directive
4. Financial or durable power of attorney

Pages 111–114 in Chapter 4 outline the purpose and meaning of living wills and advanced medical directives. These documents focus on giving your senior loved one the opportunity to spell out her wishes regarding her future medical care. They examine the type and extent of treatment measures desired should she become incapacitated and is unable to speak for herself.

A last will and testament has a different purpose. This document helps articulate how you want your property to be distributed at the time of your death. For people with children who are still minors, this is the instrument in which a guardian is appointed.

Power of Attorney

A financial or durable power of attorney (POA) addresses the question of which person or persons you've selected to help manage your assets. It allows the person you designate to act on your behalf if you are unable to manage your assets. This would occur if you had medical- or mental-incapacity problems that caused you to be unable to make responsible decisions for yourself.

If the POA is not in place and your elderly parent is suddenly incapacitated, the only option you'll have, unfortunately, is to go through court proceedings to determine who will take over this role. It can be an expensive and drawn-out process.

Another type of POA is called a "springing" power of attorney. This legal document can be implemented only when a person is deemed mentally incapacitated by a physician. The springing POA can state that incapacity must be determined by more than one doctor.

There is a significant difference between these two mechanisms. A durable POA becomes effective the moment it's signed. It remains in place regardless of the mental capacity of the person who implements it. In contrast, a springing POA only becomes effective when an individual becomes mentally incapacitated. An example of this would be a severe medical condition such as a coma or a vegetative state. It's called a "springing" POA because it essentially "springs into life" at the time of a catastrophic event.

Determining who has power of attorney is a very important decision. It should be carefully considered. The person who assumes this role must be a trusted individual who has a clear understanding of the wants and needs of your senior. He or she must be prepared to carry out the wishes stated in these documents.

Be sure to remember where the POA documents are placed; if they're needed, you don't want to waste time wondering where they are. Many people store their legal paperwork in a bank's safety-deposit box. Keep in mind that banks generally have a policy that only the box's owner and the person with POA are allowed access. You will not be allowed to retrieve the safety-deposit box unless you can prove that you have power of attorney. So do keep this document stored in a place that is accessible to the appropriate individual.

Trusts

Trusts are a popular mechanism to use in estate planning when people have a larger estate or a more complex estate. The biggest advantage in having a living trust is that the assets can be dealt with in such a way as to help minimize taxes or freeze the worth of your senior's assets, which can help decrease tax payments that must be made at the time of his death. If your parent wants to create trusts, I highly recommend that he—or you—find a lawyer with expertise in this complex specialty.

Trusts are used to transfer assets to designated individuals. This can be done while your senior is alive. Alternatively, the language of a trust can designate that its terms are executed at the time of his death.

Any assets or property placed in a trust will not be subject to probate. Probate is a process involving lawyers, judges, and court appearances, which ensures that ownership of property/assets is properly transferred from the probate estate to the designated heirs. This can be a time-consuming process that can delay the transfer of assets.

There are several different types of trusts. One of the most commonly used is called a revocable living trust. It includes the following components:

- It specifies the "grantor" or "settlor," who is the person who creates the trust.

- It includes the "trustee," the person who manages the trust and holds title to it. He or she must manage it as written in the terms of the trust.

- The grantor can be the trustee or can be a co-trustee.

- The "beneficiary" is the person or entity whom the trust designates as the recipient of the income or principal from the trust.

It is created during the grantor's lifetime and is revocable; the grantor can alter it any way she chooses during her lifetime. She can put assets in or take them out in any way she chooses.

A disadvantage of this type of trust is that the costs associated with it are greater because of its complexity. At the time of the grantor's death there are asset and document reviews, as well as transfers, that must be done. This creates more expense.

Pour-Over Will

Another important tool in estate planning is a document called a pour-over will. It's frequently used in conjunction with a revocable living trust. Its purpose is to ensure that all the property and assets that are included in the terms of a will are transferred or "poured over" into a trust at the time of the grantor's death.

There are pros and cons to using a pour-over will.

On the pro side, estate planners often recommend it because it's easy working with one document that's associated with the trust. If it's well written, it clearly states who is entitled to what. Also, they are private documents; they're not available for public scrutiny.

On the con side, property or assets in a pour-over will are subject to probate. Thus, the process can be stalled in the courts for an extended period of time, which can create higher costs and delay the distribution of property and assets into the living trust and delay their distribution to the designated recipients.

Chapter 13

The Challenges Associated with End of Life: Legal Documents, Funeral Arrangements, and More

It doesn't matter how old we are when we lose a parent. It doesn't matter if the death is sudden or slow. They will always be our parents. Even as adults we still have a parent-child relationship that helps define us and what we mean to each other.

The pain and sense of loss can feel very real at the death of a parent. Regardless of how the loss occurs, there are difficult decisions that need to be made and there are steps that must be taken. This can be particularly challenging during a time in which many of us experience intense grief and sadness.

Be sure you have easy access to key legal documents so that you can implement the estate plan per the wishes of the deceased. These documents can also facilitate your ability to pay for expenses that arose as you helped care for her. In addition, they may contain certain instruments to help cover the costs associated with a funeral and burial. Make sure you're aware of all the benefits to which beneficiaries are entitled.

In *Caring for Your Parents*, Delehanty and Ginzler list the documents that you should look for after a death. They include the following:

Insurance Policies

Your parent may have several types of insurance policies, such as life insurance, mortgage or loan insurance, medical insurance provided by an employer, or other accident insurance or credit-card insurance. The proceeds of a life insurance are paid directly to the beneficiary named on the policy and can be an important source of income for survivors left with multiple expenses. Consult a lawyer or financial advisor for options in receiving this income.

Social Security Numbers

Filing for benefits on behalf of yourself or a surviving parent will require the Social Security number of the deceased, a surviving spouse, and any dependent children. Notify the Social Security Administration of your parent's death immediately; any checks received after the death must be returned.

Military Discharge Certificate

If your parent was a veteran and you are filing for survivor or burial disability benefits, you should have a copy of a certificate of honorable (or other than dishonorable) discharge. If it isn't available, you can request a copy from the National Personnel Records Center, 1 Archive Drive, St. Louis, Mo, 63130 or you can download it from www.archives.gov/veterans.

Marriage Certificate

If the surviving parent files for any benefits, he or she will need a copy of the marriage certificate. Copies can be ordered from the county clerk records office where the original license was issued.

Birth Certificates

If these are not available for the deceased and any dependent children, copies can be ordered through the county records where your loved one was born.

Will

Your parent's written will is most likely to be kept in a safe-deposit box or among other personal papers. If the will was written with the help of a lawyer or other counsel, contact that person to see if they have a copy as well.

List of Assets

Compile a complete list of your parents' property and other assets for easy access. The list should include real estate, stocks, bonds, savings accounts, or other personal property such as automobiles or boats. A copy of your parent's most recent tax return may also be helpful.

Death Certificate

A death certificate is not something you can handle in advance, of course, but it is useful to be aware that a number of agencies will require copies of it. You will need at least five to twelve certified copies, purchased from the funeral director or local health department. If your loved one has lots of stocks or bonds or other assets, you will need a lot more copies (based on the quantity of assets) to get access to them.

Funerals: Final Conversations, Final Preparations

As the end of life approaches for your loved one, perhaps one of the most difficult challenges that must be faced is thinking about funeral or memorial arrangements. Ideally you will have had this discussion before he became ill or developed a diminished mental capacity. Many people are fearful to broach these topics because it feels uncomfortable or awkward. It may be that you don't know how your parent will feel about it.

However, for many of us, it's important to honor our parent's wishes as much as possible. If you're able to have a discussion about his special requests for honoring his memory after he has died, this may be your last chance to have this talk.

In *Caring for Your Parents*, Delehanty and Ginzler write about how being able to say good-bye represents a turning point in adult children. "Planning a funeral or memorial service in advance may seem morbid, but it can comfort everyone concerned if specific desires are spelled out ahead of time. . . . Some people like to have some kind of observance before they die, as is the tradition in a number of cultures."

The authors go on to discuss the challenges of having these final conversations. You may have to prepare yourself emotionally. And you have to weigh this opportunity against the possibility that you may have regrets leaving meaningful things forever unsaid:

> *Beyond the specifics of discussing—and not being afraid to discuss—such things as advanced directives and funeral arrangements, it's important to be prepared for the kind of thoughts and concerns that may surface during the last days of your parent's life. If your parent is still able to communicate, he may want to review his life, psychologically tying up loose ends of things done and undone. He may express wishes often in the form of final requests for loved ones to do something. And he may voice remorse. The most helpful thing you can do is listen and acknowledge*

these expressions. If a final request seems unreasonable or impossible to fulfill, don't ignore it or challenge it—but don't make false promises either. . . . Sometimes the most comforting thing you can do is say, "I understand."

When you're faced with the task of preparing a funeral for a loved one, there are several things you should consider. A funeral is a way for the living to say a final good-bye to someone they love. It can also be a critically important step in the mourning process. And for many, it can be the initial moment when healing can begin.

If you know that you're carrying out the specific wishes of your parent, this can be a source of comfort that helps make this process go as smoothly as possible.

To some it may sound strange, but there are people who plan their own funerals in advance. However, taking this kind of step can be very helpful to those who are responsible for making funeral arrangements at the time of a loved one's death. People can even pay for their own funeral ahead of time if they choose. If this is something your parent wants, inquire at your bank about something called a payable-on death (POD) or burial account. This is money set aside for funeral arrangements. There must be a specific person, or beneficiary, who is associated with this account. This instrument allows funds to be accessed immediately by the intended person to use as designated. Funeral homes expect payment at the time of the service, so preparations do need to be made at what can be a very difficult time. If arrangements can be made before death, this spares families from having to make grim and costly decisions when they're grieving.

Planning the Final Good-Bye

If your elderly loved one does have specific wishes for her funeral arrangements or memorial, encourage her to write them down, and ask her to share this information with you. This will help ensure that you have an understanding of and agreement about what will be done.

Make sure the right people know where this information is, so when the time comes it will be readily accessible. I recommend sharing it with your loved one's attorney as well.

As I've described earlier in this book, I had numerous discussions with my dad about what he wanted done at his funeral. Because he was a World War II veteran, and was active in his Veterans of Foreign Wars chapter, he wanted me to contact them at the time of his death. He told me how important it was for him to have a military funeral to honor his service to his country. He even told me the specific post to contact and what to ask them to do. He also advised me about which funeral home he wanted me to use. I was so grateful that he shared this information. It helped me to understand how much this meant to him. In turn, Dad was clearly comforted by the fact that I promised him his wishes would be carried out.

If and when you're discussing this with your senior, and he doesn't mention a specific funeral home, you may want to consider some local places. It may feel uncomfortable, but when you think about the alternative—scrambling to find someplace in the immediate aftermath of his death—it makes a lot of sense.

You'll find that funeral homes offer a range of prices and options. A reputable home should be willing to provide information about costs, packages, and professional services. Be sure to get these prices in writing. Funerals are a big business, and when you are vulnerable and grieving, you may not pay attention to what's said during the meeting with funeral directors or their staff.

Of course, you'll want to keep in mind the religious and/or cultural values of your senior when making these plans. Be sure this is included in your discussions with funeral directors. They should have information on local clergy who can participate in the funeral arrangements. This is useful if you don't have a specific person in mind. Funeral directors should also be able to make sure you have the proper death certificates. They can also assist you in making plans for an obituary.

The death certificate is an important document. You can ask for as many copies of a death certificate as you want, but be aware that you'll be charged for each copy you have made. If your loved one has multiple bank accounts, insurance policies, and/or multiple stock investments, you'll need a corresponding number of death certificates. When you begin the work of executing an estate plan following your loved one's death, you'll be asked to present a death certificate as part of the process. Banks, insurance companies, and stock companies cannot legally work with you without this documentation.

As I touched on above, people have different religious beliefs and/or values; this will impact what they want to happen when they die. There are three main options to consider when determining how and where the remains of a loved one will ultimately go:

Burial

This means that a cemetery plot must be bought. You must have a casket for the burial, and the casket must be placed in either a vault or some type of liner which is placed in the grave surrounding the casket. Cemeteries generally require you to have some type of headstone or grave marker. Each cemetery has its own rules and regulations about this.

Cremation

This is a process during which the body is burned and the ashes are preserved. The question then becomes what to do with the ashes. They can be placed in a special container called an urn, or kept in a box. Many people request that their ashes be scattered in a place that holds special meaning for them. Funeral directors will know about any laws prohibiting the scattering of ashes in certain locations.

Entombment

Another option is to have your senior's body placed in a mausoleum or tomb. The casket is placed above ground in a freestanding building which functions as a monument to the memory of the deceased. Mausoleums can hold one or several people. Some mausoleums are public. Or, given the appropriate financial resources, it can be private. Some mausoleums are located in cemeteries; others are built to stand alone in a specified place that has special meaning for the deceased and/or their family.

Do you want to have flowers at your loved one's funeral? Or would donations be a more appropriate choice? Perhaps there is a charity or organization which has special significance to your senior and/or your family. You can state your preferences, if any, in the obituary or at the funeral service or memorial.

Your funeral director will ask you to decide about several things. For example, do you want the casket to be open so that the body of the deceased can be seen? He or she will also ask whether or not you want the casket or urn present at the service. Your answers may be based on religious beliefs or very personal values. Depending on your situation, you may want to discuss these choices with close family or other appropriate people before making a final decision.

You have the option to include a funeral or memorial service immediately after your loved one is buried, or you can schedule it for a later date. This allows you to make any special preparations; it can also allow additional time for mourning. If there are others helping you make these arrangements, this is another topic you may want to discuss with them.

Your deceased loved one may be eligible for government funds to help pay for the costs of these services. These funds are limited but can help offset some expenses. The Social Security Administration offers a lump-sum death payment of $255 if specific eligibility criteria is met. For example, a surviving spouse must be living in the household of the deceased at the time of his/her death. Survivors must apply for this money within two years of the death. For more information, visit the Social Security Administration website at www.ssa.gov or call 800-722-1213.

The Veterans Administration (VA) will also offer a small allowance of up to $300 for the burial and/or funeral expenses of a former veteran for a non-service-related death. To learn more, contact the VA at 800-827-1000 or go to its website at www.benefits.va.gov/BENEFITS/factsheets/burials/Burial.pdf. Another option is the National Cemetery Administration at www.cem.va.gov/cem/burial_benefits.

Dividing Possessions after a Loved One Dies

One of the most challenging tasks after the death of a loved one can be deciding how her possessions will be dispersed. Family relationships have been destroyed over this. Many times there is no written documentation indicating who should receive what items. This leaves it up to the remaining family to make this determination. There is no sole right or wrong way to make these decisions. What do you do if two or more people are passionate about keeping a specific item? What if one person wants many expensive items?

One way to avoid this problem is to discuss it with your loved one while she is alive and thinking clearly. She can individually spend time with family members discussing items in the estate, describing their history and worth, and directly asking what they'd like to have someday. The sharing of this history can offer an opportunity to explain why an item has special significance to the person giving it. It can enhance the relationship between a senior and the future heirs.

There may be reasons why a particular item means more to one family member than another. Maybe an item was purchased on a trip with a loved one and there is sentimental value for that person who wishes to keep it after the loved one dies. Sometimes one family member may have more financial need than others, and there is agreement that this person should get a larger part of an estate.

Here again, it may feel awkward, even daunting, to initiate this discussion with your parent. However, it has the potential to avoid lots of friction and disagreements that may lie ahead if these wishes are not clarified and put in writing in a will. If possible, make sure the will clarifies why a particular individual is given a specific item.

My dad shared his will with me. Regarding certain decisions he'd made, I felt it was important that he explain them in his own words so that when the time came, all of my siblings knew his thought process. I felt it was vital that the words came from him and not from me. I discussed this with my dad and he agreed it was important. He included this information in his will.

My husband's family was very creative in the way they handled this process among themselves. Steve's parents went around the house, describing the items they wanted dispersed after their deaths. They mentioned where and how they were acquired, and the sentimental value they contained. They enjoyed collecting folk art, and it was really helpful for us to understand the value and origin of each item and learn about the artists and their work.

There were some items in the house that, before their parents died, a few family members expressed interest in having. Here's how they handled it. They all walked through the house with different-colored stickers. Anyone who was interested in a piece of jewelry, artwork, furniture, or other item placed a sticker on it. If there were multiple stickers on a particular item, the family members involved talked about it and worked it out between themselves.

Steve has seven siblings, and even with all of these people involved there wasn't any conflict in the end. This process does involve compromise at times. But it can be very effective. It helps you determine which items have special significance for you. It also gives you the chance to really think about what feels right for you to have and why.

For families that can't physically be together, an inventory with pictures can be made and distributed electronically.

There are a variety of ways these inheritance decisions can be made. You can match an item to a person's area of interest. For example, a family member who is a musician may want to take a piano that is left in an estate. You can each take a turn selecting an item. In a situation like this, you may want to divide items into categories. Items to be inherited can be divided by their financial value, for example, or by their sentimental value.

Identifying and Locating Assets

Many seniors are continually acquiring possessions. Conversely, some decide to downsize. The value of liquid assets, stocks and bonds, and/or property can change quickly. Make sure that the information in your loved one's will or estate-planning distribution is as current as possible. Ideally, everyone who's involved will clearly understand the parameters and contents of the estate.

Someone should write down the list of items and document what decisions have been made about who is going to get what. This information should be kept in a safe place. It's a good idea to make copies for the people who are directly impacted by the inheritance of the items.

Sometimes family members have a contentious relationship and are unable to make inheritance decisions in a reasonable, thoughtful way. If this is the situation in your family, you can hire a mediator or legal expert who specializes in estate planning or inheritance issues to help resolve these difficult conflicts.

Chapter 14

Additional Caregiver Resources

In previous chapters you'll have found a variety of tips and resources to help you care for your aging loved one. In this chapter, you'll find still more. Several provide very helpful information and support for the caregiver. Also, you may be interested in the programs that offer caregivers an opportunity to connect with others in the same situation, fostering an exchange of ideas, experiences, and new resources. Sometimes, if you're feeling isolated, making an emotional connection with someone in a similar role can really help. This type of alliance can also affirm that the things you are doing, the feelings you have, and the challenges you are facing are not unusual.

Nationwide Caregiver Support Resources

- To find a caregiver support group, contact your local hospital and speak with a staff social worker.

- Contact your local agency on aging.

- Contact your local senior center.

Use the Eldercare Locator, a public service of the US Administration on Aging, to find services for older adults and their families at: www.eldercare.gov, or call them at: 800-677-1116.

- Family Caregiver Alliance's National Center on Caregiving offers research and advocacy for family caregiving, available online at: www.caregiver.org/national-center-caregiving. The Alliance also has a webinar site where you'll find video teaching sessions to get information on "Seasons of Care: Wellness and Self-Care for the Family Caregiver" at: www.caregiver.org/seasons-care-wellness-and-self-care-family-caregiver.

- National Alliance for Caregiving provides research and advocacy. Available online at: www.caregiving.org.

- ElderCare Online offers information and support for people who are taking care of aging family: www.ec-online.net.

- Family caregiver seminars and information are offered via AARP. Visit the Caregiving Resource Center at https://secure.aarp.org/home-family/caregiving/?cmp=RDRCT-CRGVGRECNT_JUN22_012.

- The United Hospital Fund offers caregiver resource information via its Next Step in Care site: www.nextstepincare.org/.

- Caring.com offers assisted-living, independent-living, in-home-care, and caregiving resources at: www.caring.com and 800-952-6650.

- Veterans Administration Caregiver Support helps you connect with, and access, caregiver support services at your local VA. Call their Caregiver Support Line at: 855-260-3274, or visit their website at: www.caregiver.va.gov/support/support_services.asp.

- The Senior Services Caregiver Program offers a printable online brochure, classes, resources, informational videos, and other good information. You can call them at:

888-4ELDERS (888-435-3377) or visit
them online at: www.seniorservices.org/
caregiving/home.aspx.

State Caregiver Support Resources

* Volunteers of America Caregiver Services
  in Minnesota's services include assistance
  for people over sixty who are suffering
  from Alzheimer's disease, chronic health
  conditions, or frailty. Call 952-945-4000 or
  go online to: www.voamnwi.org/Minnesota.

* The "Caring for Your Parents: Caregiver
  Resources and Caregiver Handbook" offers
  information on a variety of caregiving
  topics. The website is: www.pbs.org/
  wgbh/caringforyourparents/handbook/
  caringcaregiver/supportgroups.html.

* Genesee County, New York, offers caregiver
  support services including resource and
  support group information. Call 585-
  343-1611 or visit their website at: www.
  co.genesee.ny.us/departments/office_for_
  the_aging/caregiver_support_services.html.

* Humana offers a "caregiver toolkit" with tips

for facing the challenges of caregiving. You can find it on their website at: www.humana.com/individual-and-family-support/caregivers/.

- The Illinois Department on Aging offers a host of resources via its Family Caregiver Support Program. The website is: www.illinois.gov/aging/CommunityServices/caregiver/Pages/caregiver_links.aspx.

- The Kentucky Cabinet for Health and Family Services has a web page filled with helpful programs and services at: www.chfs.ky.gov/dail/Programs.htm.

- In Michigan, the Office of Services to the Aging has a Caregiver Resource Center full of support and service information. Call 517-373-8230 or go to the website at: www.michigan.gov/osa/1,4635,7-234-64083_64551---,00.html.

- The state of Oregon site has information on local and national caregiving resources at: www.oregon.gov/dhs/spwpd/pages/caregiving/nfcs.aspx or call the Oregon Department of Human Services at: 503-945-5811.

- The state of Arizona offers caregiver program information through its Department of

Economic Security at https://des.az.gov, which also provides links to other resources such as the Area Agency on Aging at: www. aaaphx.org, and the Caregiver Resources Line at: 1-888-737-7494 and Arizona adult protective services.

- The state of Utah offers caregiver and senior services information through its Aging and Adult Services website at: at http://www. hsdaas.utah.gov/.

- MedlinePlus offers information on caregiving tasks such as bathing, moving, lifting patients, and much more. Visit it at: www.nlm.nih.gov/medlineplus/ caregivers.html.

Caregiver Wellness Information

- This caregiver support website offers information on how the caretaker can stay well: www.caring.com/caregiver-wellness.

- Information on defining the caretaker role, identifying potential caretaker health risks, and self-care options for caretakers can be found at: www.familydoctor.org/

familydoctor/en/seniors/caregiving/
caregiver-health-and-wellness.html.

- The Mid-East Area Agency on Aging in
  Missouri offers support services and resources.
  Learn more at its website: www.mid-eastaaa.
  org/arc_caregiver_wellness.php.

- The Alzheimer's Support Network of
  Naples, Florida, has a host of articles on
  caretaker-related topics. Learn more at its
  website: www.alzsupport.org/Caregiver_
  Wellness.html.

- A series of articles about caregiver wellness
  topics is available at: www.examiner.com/
  topic/caregiver-wellness.

Geriatric Care Managers

- The national office of Aging Life Care
  Associates, formerly known as the National
  Association of Private Geriatric Care Managers, can be found at: 3275 W. Ina Road,
  Suite 130, Tucson, AZ, 85741-2198. The
  phone number is: 520-881-8008, and the
  national website is: www.aginglifecare.org.

- The New England Chapter of Aging Life Care Association encompasses Connecticut, Rhode Island, Maine, Massachusetts, New Hampshire, Vermont, and Quebec, Canada. Its website offers resource information for caregivers, help finding geriatric care managers, and more at: www.gcmnewengalnd.org.

- The Mid-Atlantic Professional Geriatric Care Managers includes Delaware, Virginia, West Virginia, Pennsylvania, Maryland, and Washington, DC: www.midatlanticgcm.org/.

- The *New York Times* blog by Jane Gross titled "Why Hire a Geriatric Care Manager?" is available online at: www.newoldage. blogs.nytimes.com/2008/10/06/why-hire-a-geriatric-care-manager/?_r=0.

- The National Care Planning Council has a website listing state-by-state information on eldercare services and geriatric care managers at: www.longtermcarelink.net/a2bfind-manager.htm.

- The website of the Alzheimer's Association has an article with lots of good information on geriatric care managers, including how to interview them and questions to think about at: www.alz.org/stl/documents/gcm_tips.pdf.

- The Midwest Chapter of Professional Geriatric Care Managers includes Illinois, Indiana, Iowa, Kansas, Kentucky, Michigan, Minnesota, Missouri, Nebraska, North Dakota, Ohio, South Dakota, Wisconsin, and Ontario, Canada. It is available online at: www.aginglifecare.org/ALCA/Regional_Chapters/Midwest_Chapter/ALCA/Regional_Chapters/Midwest_Chapter/Midwest_Chapter_Home_Page.aspx. This site also offers links to chapters in Florida, New Jersey, New York, and more.

Veteran Resources

Veterans and family members are eligible for financial relief and additional help.

- The VFW offers numerous discounts including a prescription discount. Information is available online at: www.vfw.org/Join/New-Member-Benefits/Medical-Services/.

- The US Department of Veteran Affairs has a website called VA Caregiver Support, which offers good resource information that can help connect you with caretakers, programs

near your home, and more at: www.caregiver.
va.gov/ or call: 855-260-3274.

- Contact the Veterans Administration
  to learn about health-benefits eligibility.
  Call 877-222-8387 or go online at: www.
  va.gov/healthbenefits/resources/Caregiver_
  Eligibility_Check.asp.

- The website www.military.com has
  information about available benefits for
  caregiver programs and services at: www.
  military.com/benefits/veterans-health-care/
  veteran-benefits-caregiver-programs-and-
  services.html.

- The website www.agingcare.com has
  information regarding VA financial support
  for caregivers, as well as links to get more
  information about caring for people with
  dementia and Alzheimer's disease, and
  finding help for non-family caregivers. Go
  to: www.agingcare.com/Veterans-Assistance.

- Philips's Lifeline offers a web page with
  information about "Military Caregivers
  Have Many Options for Support," along
  with additional resource information at:
  www.lifeline.philips.com

- The Veterans Crisis Line is 800-273-8255. Callers can simply press "1" on their phones to be connected with a person who can offer confidential help and resource information. The website is: www.veteranscrisisline.net/forfamilyandfriends.aspx.

- The Department of Defense Office of Warrior Care Policy offers a host of resources available to veterans, their families, and caregivers at: http://warriorcare.dodlive.mil.

Medicare Savings Programs

- Medicare offers programs that can provide some financial relief for those who are eligible. Find out more at the websites listed below.

- For more information on help in paying for insurance premiums, copays, and prescriptions, go to: www.medicare.gov/your-medicare-costs/help-paying-costs/save-on-drug-costs/save-on-drug-costs.html.

- Medicare Interactive is a free, independent online resource that helps answer questions about your Medicare benefits and rights. It

can be found at: www.medicareinteractive.
org/page2.php.

• The National Council on Aging has
created a website called Medicare Matters,
which helps answer questions relating to
Medicare coverage. It can be found at: www.
mymedicarematters.org/costs/getting-help-
with-costs/.

Legal Resources

As I mentioned in Chapters 9, 12, and 13, there are many
situations in which an aging senior requires the services of
an attorney to help ensure that all the proper legal documentation is in place when needed. Elder law is a specialty
area that specifically addresses these issues.

• The National Academy of Elder Law
Attorneys can help you find attorneys
specializing in elder law as well as advocacy
groups; it offers helpful publications as well.
Call 703-942-5711 or visit its website at:
www.naela.org.

• The American Bar Association has a website
offering information about elder issues,
including guardianship, durable power of

attorney, bank fraud, and much more at:
www.americanbar.org/groups/law_aging/
resources.html.

• The website located at www.
estateplanninglinks.com/about.html was
created by an attorney, and offers many
helpful articles about estate planning, as well
as links to additional resources and sample
copies of valuable documents needed for
estate planning.

• Compiled by several attorneys specializing
in elder law, the site located at www.
elderlawanswers.com/about-us offers useful
information about Medicare and Medicaid
benefits, estate planning, guardianship, and
other legal concerns that affect seniors.

Resources for the Elderly Who Live at Home

There are unique challenges that arise when an aging senior
begins to have medical, physical, or memory problems but
chooses to remain at home. These resources offer information to both enhance safety, and help with management of
day-to-day care and activities.

- To help determine if your senior loved
  one's home is safe, here's a comprehensive
  checklist of considerations: www.
  aplaceformom.com/senior-care-resources/
  articles/elderly-home-safety-checklist.

- The "Aging Parents and Elder Care" website
  offers a lot of information on a wide range
  of topics including "Daily Living Solutions,"
  eldercare support groups, checklists, books,
  videos, and resource information at: www.
  aging-parents-and-elder-care.com.

- The www.helpguide.org website has good
  information about "Home Care Services
  for Seniors," with resources to help make
  decisions about staying at home or not,
  household maintenance, transportation,
  connecting seniors with home-care services,
  and much more. This site was started by a
  couple who lost their twenty-nine-year-old
  daughter to depression and suicide. They put
  together a team of professional experts to
  help people of all ages cope with a variety of
  problems relating to mental and emotional
  health issues. There is good resource
  material on programs nationwide. The
  site can be found at: www.helpguide.org/
  articles/senior-housing/home-care-services-
  for-seniors.htm.

Notes

Introduction

According to the 2010 census: US Census Bureau, 2010 Census Special Reports, *Centenarians: 2010, C2010SR-03,* US Government Printing Office, Washington, DC, 2012, Introduction, p. 1.

A study by the Gerontology Research Group: Gerontology Research Group, "Current Validated Living Supercentenarians" as of November 13, 2014.

They reported that this "is especially prevalent . . .": Pew Research Center, Internet, Science, and Tech, "Family Caregivers Are Wired for Health," by Susannah Fox, Maeve Duggan, and Kristen Purcell, June 20, 2013, www. pewinternet.org/2013/06/20/family-caregivers-are-wired-for-health/.

The Pew Research Center reports: Pew Research Center, Internet, Science, and Tech, "Family Caregivers Are Wired for Health," by Susannah Fox, Maeve Duggan, and Kristen Purcell, June 20, 2013, www.pewinternet.org/2013/06/20/family-caregivers-are-wired-for-health/.

Chapter 1

In their book *Caring for Your Parents*: *Caring for Your Parents: The Complete Family Guide*, by Hugh Delehanty and Elinor Ginzler, Sterling Publishing Company, 2010, p. 160.

The American Psychological Association (APA): The American Psychological Association, "Grief: Coping with the Loss of Your Loved One," was adapted from a post by Katherine C. Nordal, PhD, on the APA's "Your Mind Your Body" blog, March 2011, at: www.apa.org/helpcenter/grief.aspx.

Chapter 2

The National Institutes of Health defines dementia: US National Library of Medicine, National Institutes of Health, Medline Plus, "Dementia," Luc Jasmin, MD, PhD, September 26, 2011, at: www.nlm.nih.gov/medlineplus/ency/article/000739.htm.

According to gerontologist Cheryl Kuba: *Navigating the Journey of Aging Parents: What Care Receivers Want* by Cheryl Kuba, Routledge Publishing, 2006, p. 53.

Here are some things to do: Mayo Clinic, "Memory Loss: Seven Tips to Improve Your Memory," by Mayo Clinic staff, March 5, 2014, available online at: www.mayoclinic. org/healthy-living/healthy-aging/in-depth/memory-loss/ art-20046518.

You can expect the physician to ask: Mayo Clinic, "Reversible Causes of Memory Loss," by Mayo Clinic staff, November 22, 2014, available online at: http://www. mayoclinic.org/diseases-conditions/alzheimers-disease/ in-depth/memory-loss/art-20046326?pg=2.

Darby Morhardt, MSW, LCSW, PhD, has been working with Alzheimer's patients: CNN Living, "Building Relationships Amid Memory Loss," by Sarah LeTrent, April 9, 2012, www.cnn.com/2012/04/09/living/dementia-building -relationships/.

Spouses and adult children can be confused: CNN Living, "Building Relationships Amid Memory Loss," by Sarah LeTrent, April 9, 2012, www.cnn.com/2012/04/09/living/ dementia-building-relationships/.

Chapter 4

If you find yourself in a similarly challenging situation: *Caring for Your Parents: The Complete AARP Guide* by Hugh Delehanty and Elinor Ginzler, Sterling Publishing Company, 2005, p.160.

Authors Delehanty and Ginzler offer these suggestions: *Caring for Your Parents: The Complete AARP Guide* by Hugh Delehanty and Elinor Ginzler, Sterling Publishing Company, 2005, p.159.

When you spend a lot of time around someone: *Caring for Your Parents: The Complete AARP Guide* by Hugh Delehanty and Elinor Ginzler, Sterling Publishing Company, 2005, p. 163.

When your loved one is close to death: *Caring for Your Parents: The Complete AARP Guide* by Hugh Delehanty and Elinor Ginzler, Sterling Publishing Company, 2005, p. 166.

Chapter 5

The American Association of Retired Persons (AARP) publishes a useful checklist: AARP, Home and Family, Getting Around, "Ten Signs That It's Time to Limit or Stop Driving," by AARP Driver Safety, January 2010, available online at: www.aarp.org/home-garden/transportation/info-05-2010/Warning_Signs_Stopping.html.

In *Caring for Your Parents*, authors Hugh Delehanty and Elinor Ginzler offer these recommendations: *Caring for Your Parents: The Complete AARP Guide* by Hugh Delehanty and Elinor Ginzler, Sterling Publishing Company, 2005, p.153.

In *How to Care for Aging Parents*, **Virginia Morris offers helpful information:** *How to Care for Aging Parents* by Virginia Morris, Workman Publishing, 2004, pp. 105–106.

If you're considering hiring a caregiver: *Navigating the Journey of Aging Parents: What Care Receivers Want* by Cheryl Kuba, Routledge Publishing, 2006, p. 99.

Chapter 7

When you visit your aging parents: *The Eldercare Handbook: Different Choices, Compassionate Solutions* by Stella Mora Henry, RN, William Morrow Paperbacks/HarperCollins, 2006, p. 15.

Henry also describes the behaviors: *The Eldercare Handbook: Different Choices, Compassionate Solutions* by Stella Mora Henry, RN, William Morrow Paperbacks/HarperCollins, 2006, p. 29.

In their book *Caring for Your Parents*: *Caring for Your Parents: The Complete Family Guide* by Hugh Delehanty and Elinor Ginzler, Sterling Publishing Company, 2010, p. 21.

In *Caring for Your Parents*, **Delehanty and Ginzler:** *Caring for Your Parents: The Complete AARP Guide* by Hugh Delehanty and Elinor Ginzler, Sterling Publishing Company, 2005, p. 23.

Chapter 9

Be sure that you know all the providers: *Caring for Your Parents: The Complete AARP Guide* by Hugh Delehanty and Elinor Ginzler, Sterling Publishing Company, 2005, p. 42.

Chapter 10

Unfortunately, there are all kinds of scams that unscrupulous people use: "Identity Theft," US Government, April 25, 2014, www.usa.gov/topics/money/identity-theft/prevention.shtml.

Chapter 11

Here are some important aspects related to nursing-home care: Medicare, "How Can I Pay for Nursing Home Care?" available online at: www.medicare.gov/what-medicare-covers/part-a/paying-for-nursing-home-care.html.

In *The Eldercare Handbook*, Stella Mora Henry offers these additional tips: *The Eldercare Handbook: Different Choices, Compassionate Solutions* by Stella Mora Henry, RN, William Morrow Paperbacks/HarperCollins, 2006, p. 135.

Chapter 12

According to *Forbes* magazine: *Forbes,* "Estate Planning for Seniors Should Be Done Before a Life-Changing Event," by Bernard A. Krooks, October 19, 2011, www.forbes.com/sites/bernardkrooks/2011/10/19/estate-planning-for-seniors-should-be-done-before-a-life-changing-event/.

Chapter 13

In *Caring for Your Parents*, Hugh Delehanty and Elinor Ginzler list the documents: *Caring for Your Parents: The Complete AARP Guide* by Hugh Delehanty and Elinor Ginzler, Sterling Publishing, 2005, p.168.

In *Caring for Your Parents*, Delehanty and Ginzler: *Caring for Your Parents: The Complete AARP Guide* by Hugh Delehanty and Elinor Ginzler, Sterling Publishing, 2005, p. 161.

The authors go on to discuss the challenges: *Caring for Your Parents: The Complete AARP Guide* by Hugh Delehanty and Elinor Ginzler, Sterling Publishing, 2005, pp.161–162.

Acknowledgments

When I decided to write this book, I discussed it with my dad to make sure he was on board with it. I felt it was wrong to tell his life story without his input and permission. Happily, he agreed.

I quickly realized this was a family story. I could not tell my dad's story without sharing very personal aspects of the lives of myself, my brother, Danny, and my sisters, Susie and Caryn. I want to begin by thanking all of them for honoring me with their trust and support in allowing me to share some of our most private family moments. I would not have written this book without their sanction and support.

Blending my father's story, using his words and mine, while providing a narrative for caregivers was a complicated task. This book is an unusual hybrid. On top of that, there were additional challenges associated with being objective and sensitive regarding the telling of the story of our family. None of this would have been possible without the guidance and writing skills of my editor, Lisa Pliscou. She was a joy to collaborate with. She helped me to craft the book I dreamed of creating. Her sensitivity regarding the content of this book and what it meant to me is something I will always be grateful for.

It is my belief that consulting experts on key topics when writing a book that offers "how to" information holds great value. I want to extend my appreciation to Fred Weber for his legal expertise, and Edie, RN, for allowing me to interview her. They generously shared their time, knowledge, and professional and personal experience with me. This helped ensure my readers would have the best possible advice on estate planning and finding the right assisted living program.

Thanks to She Writes Press, and Brooke Warner, for seeing the value in my work and its potential to reach many others. Her support team, especially project manager Lauren Wise and designer Julie Metz, helped create the final product you have in front of you. Thanks to Taylor Vargecko, my publicist. I am grateful to them for their time, energy, and expertise.

Blair Holmes took photographs of me for this book. He shared his time and photographic talents. I wanted to thank you for your generosity, Blair.

I am also grateful for the wonderful testimonials from Sue Gartzman, Susan Alterman, PsyD, and Nina McKissock, RN, and Susan Johnson Hadler. Thank you for your kind words.

Finally, I also wanted to thank Steven Atkinson, PA-C, MS. I attended a conference two years ago where he presented. I was in awe of his wisdom and knowledge about working with the aging population and their loved ones. He had a passion for it. I spoke with him and told him I hoped to write a book about elderly people and their loved ones and asked if he would be willing to take a look at it and comment. He readily agreed, sensing we had similar philosophies and reverence for these people. You are a man of your word, Steven. I am so grateful to you for making the time to read my work, and for reacting to it as you did. That meant a lot to me. I can't tell you how much I appreciate it.

About the Author

Iris Waichler has been a licensed clinical social worker for over 30 years with 13 years of experience working in hospitals. Ms. Waichler has done workshops, individual, and group counseling with people experiencing infertility, strokes, cancer, and a variety of catastrophic illnesses.

She has also authored 3 books. All of these books have an advocacy theme. Her first book was *Patient Power: How to Have a Say During Your Hospital Stay.* She co-authored her second book, *A Book is Born.* Ms. Waichler's third book,

Riding the Infertility Roller Coaster: A Guide to Educate and Inspire, was the recipient of multiple book awards including the Mom's Choice Award for best book of the year and the National Association of Parenting Publications (NAPPA) best book of the year.

Ms. Waichler has authored hundreds of articles on health, patient, and family advocacy topics. Ms. Waichler has done freelance writing for Demand Media, examiner. com, The American Fertility Association/path2parenthood. org and, fertilityauthority.com.

Her website is http://iriswaichler.wpengine.com/

Iris lives in Chicago with her husband, Steve, daughter, Grace, and her dog Brandi.

Author photo by Blair Holmes

SELECTED TITLES FROM SHE WRITES PRESS

She Writes Press is an independent publishing company founded to serve women writers everywhere. Visit us at www.shewritespress.com.

Falling Together: How to Find Balance, Joy, and Meaningful Change When Your Life Seems to be Falling Apart by Donna Cardillo. $16.95, 978-1-63152-077-8. A funny, big-hearted self-help memoir that tackles divorce, caregiving, burnout, major illness, fears, and low self-esteem—and explores the renewal that comes when we are able to meet these challenges with courage.

From Sun to Sun: A Hospice Nurse's Reflection on the Art of Dying by Nina Angela McKissock. $16.95, 978-1-63152-808-8. Weary from the fear people have of talking about the process of dying and death, a highly experienced registered nurse takes the reader into the world of twenty-one of her beloved patients as they prepare to leave this earth.

The Space Between: A Memoir of Mother-Daughter Love at the End of Life by Virginia A. Simpson. $16.95, 978-1-63152-049-5. When a life-threatening illness makes it necessary for Virginia Simpson's mother, Ruth, to come live with her, Simpson struggles to heal their relationship before Ruth dies.

Green Nails and Other Acts of Rebellion: Life After Loss by Elaine Soloway. $16.95, 978-1-63152-919-1. An honest, often humorous account of the joys and pains of caregiving for a loved one with a debilitating illness.

The Shelf Life of Ashes: A Memoir by Hollis Giammatteo. $16.95, 978-1-63152-047-1. Confronted by an importuning mother 3,000 miles away who thinks her end is nigh—and feeling ambushed by her impending middle age—Giammatteo determines to find The Map of Aging Well, a decision that leads her on an often-comic journey.

Don't Leave Yet: How My Mother's Alzheimer's Opened My Heart by Constance Hanstedt. $16.95, 978-1-63152-952-8. The chronicle of Hanstedt's journey toward independence, self-assurance, and connectedness as she cares for her mother, who is rapidly losing her own identity to the early stage of Alzheimer's.